The 24-Hour TV Pilot with ChatGPT

Andrew Parry

Published by Andrew Parry, 2025.

THE 24-HOUR TV PILOT WITH CHATGPT

First edition. April 28, 2025.

ISBN: 979-8231190225

Written by Andrew Parry.

Table of Contents

How to Write a Pilot for a TV Series in One Day with ChatGPT

Let's be honest. The idea of writing a pilot episode for a TV series in one day sounds completely nuts. In the traditional world of screenwriting, pilots can take weeks or even months to get right. There are brainstorming sessions, character bios, multiple drafts, peer reviews, rewrites, and then some. But here you are, wondering if it's even possible to pull it off in a single day. Not only is it possible—it's practical. And with the right mindset, tools, and a little help from artificial intelligence, you can absolutely do it.

This book isn't about cutting corners or churning out something that feels cheap or rushed. It's about unlocking creative flow, eliminating bottlenecks, and using ChatGPT to its fullest potential as your on-demand writing partner. The kind of partner who doesn't get tired, doesn't judge, and is always ready to brainstorm, plot, structure, rewrite, and throw out ideas at lightning speed. Whether you're a total beginner or a seasoned screenwriter looking to fast-track your ideas, this book will walk you through how to take a concept and turn it into a tightly written pilot script—all in a single focused day.

So why start with the pilot? Because the pilot is the DNA of your TV series. It sets the tone, introduces your characters, outlines the world, and hints at the series arc. It's also the script that determines whether anyone—be it an audience, agent, producer, or streaming platform—wants to see more. If the pilot doesn't land, nothing else matters. This first episode is your golden ticket to capturing attention and generating interest in your story.

But here's the thing: starting a pilot can be the hardest part. You might have a killer idea or a character that keeps showing up in your dreams, but when you sit down to write, you freeze. Where do you begin? Do you outline first? Write the ending? Create a world bible? That's where this book comes in. We're going to strip away the chaos and give you a clear, efficient path to getting your story on the page. We'll show you how to start with the end in mind and work backwards to make sure your plot has purpose. We'll tap into ChatGPT to generate structure, deepen character motivation, punch up your dialogue, and even throw unexpected twists into your scenes when your own brain feels like mush.

ChatGPT isn't just a tool for writing lines—it's a creative partner. It can help you refine your ideas, ask you smart questions, and provide endless possibilities to explore until you find the right one. It's not here to replace you, it's here to elevate you. This book will show you exactly how to have those conversations with the AI in ways that feel natural and collaborative. It's not about spoon-feeding prompts—it's about learning to think dynamically with your co-writer.

We're also going to go beyond the script itself. A pilot needs context. We'll cover how to pitch the show, what to include in your series bible, how to think like a showrunner, and how to present your pilot as part of a larger vision. The end goal isn't just to write a script. The end goal is to create something that sells, that connects with audiences, and that you can build a whole world around.

And yes, we'll be moving fast. But speed doesn't mean sacrificing quality—it means making decisions with confidence. We'll teach you how to trust your instincts and lean on ChatGPT when you need to push through a block or test out new ideas in seconds. You'll learn how to generate scenes, restructure a slow second act, or bring a flat character to life—all on the fly.

By the time you finish this book, you'll know how to write a complete pilot script in one sitting, and more importantly, you'll know how to repeat the process. You'll develop a rhythm, a method, and a mindset that turns you from an "aspiring writer" into someone who actually gets things done. You'll start thinking in episodes. In arcs. In hooks and cliffhangers. And every time you open a new ChatGPT window, you'll see a blank page not as something to fear, but as something to play with.

So grab a coffee, fire up your laptop, and get ready to write. Whether it's your first pilot or your tenth, you're about to learn how to create something incredible—with the help of one very patient, very brilliant AI partner.

Let's begin.

Starting with the End: The Secret to Writing a Great Pilot

If there's one secret that separates professional screenwriters from those endlessly rewriting their first ten pages, it's this: they start with the end. It's not about guessing where the story *might* go. It's about knowing *exactly* where it lands—and then reverse-engineering everything so the journey feels inevitable, yet still surprising. The pilot might be the beginning of your series, but it should echo the climax of the final episode. Everything you write in that very first scene should be pointing the audience toward a story arc that concludes with emotional and narrative payoff. That's how you craft a pilot with purpose. That's how you get people hooked.

Starting with the end allows you to write with intent instead of wandering through scenes and hoping it all makes sense later. With ChatGPT, this approach becomes even more effective because you can clearly describe your desired destination and then use the AI to brainstorm logical and compelling ways to arrive there. When you know what your finale looks like—who your protagonist becomes, what's at stake, and what's resolved—you gain a kind of storytelling compass. And every single scene in your pilot becomes a stepping stone toward that destination.

So what does this look like in practice? You begin by imagining the last episode of the season—or even the series. What has changed? Who has evolved? What has been lost, gained, destroyed, or redeemed? You might write a quick scene summary or even have ChatGPT generate a closing monologue or climactic showdown. The point is to make that ending real in your mind. It doesn't have to be perfect. It just has to exist. With that vision in place, the pilot transforms into a machine designed to launch the trajectory toward that specific endpoint.

Let's say you're writing a crime thriller series. Your endgame might be a morally compromised detective forced to kill their former partner to stop a larger conspiracy. Now go back to your pilot. That same detective should be introduced with traits that, in hindsight, make that ending make sense. Maybe they're idealistic, by-the-book, and trust their partner completely. That contrast is what gives your story a strong arc. It also allows you to layer irony, tension, and foreshadowing into the pilot from the very first scene.

This strategy works across all genres. Writing a sitcom? Think about the long-term relationship dynamics between your characters. Writing a sci-fi epic? Define the eventual world-altering event and work backwards to the small moment that sparks it. Writing a coming-of-age drama? Figure out what "grown-up" decision the character makes at the end, then show them as the opposite in the pilot. It's like setting a GPS—you'll still take creative turns and hit unexpected bumps, but you'll always know where you're going.

Now here's where ChatGPT becomes your co-pilot in the most literal sense. You can tell it the final outcome you want, and it can help you build the road back to the beginning. You can ask it to generate backstory, motivations, rivalries, or even the cause-and-effect chain that leads from episode one to the series finale. This gives you a map before you've even written a line of dialogue. And once you have that map, you can start writing your pilot with real momentum and clarity.

This method also helps eliminate a lot of common pilot-writing problems. Writers often struggle with pilots because they try to do too much—introduce every character, explain the world, set up multiple plotlines—without knowing what really matters to the bigger story. But when you know your ending, you can be ruthless about what to include and what to save for later. You stop throwing in random characters or subplots just because they seem interesting in the moment. You start building a cohesive foundation that actually supports the weight of the story you're about to tell.

Let's look at a practical example. Suppose your end scene is a quiet moment between two enemies who have become allies, sitting in the ruins of a world they both helped destroy. That's evocative, right? Now you go to the pilot and think: what's the opposite of that? Maybe the opening scene is a loud, flashy standoff where they're trying to kill each other. Maybe they don't even know each other yet, but they're on a collision course. Either way, you've just given yourself a beautiful contrast, and your entire series can be about how these two people change and what that says about the world you've built.

The audience doesn't need to know the end. But they need to *feel* that your story is going somewhere. That's the energy you tap into when you write your pilot from the end backwards. It's the reason why some pilots feel like they're meandering and others feel like they're tight and purposeful, even if you don't understand everything yet. The latter kind is the one that gets picked up. It's the kind that has networks and streaming execs asking, "What happens next?"

And that brings us to the final, very real benefit of this approach: speed. You're here because you want to write a pilot in one day, not one month. Starting with the end dramatically reduces your decision-making time. You stop second-guessing whether a scene belongs, because you know if it supports the overall arc. You stop writing scenes just to fill pages, because every beat is designed to plant a seed that pays off later. You'll move faster because you're moving with direction.

Using ChatGPT to write a pilot in one day doesn't mean you're rushing. It means you're leveraging your imagination and AI's power to streamline the creative process. When you begin with the ending, you're not improvising your way through a script—you're constructing it with intention. You're not hoping for magic to strike on page 35. You're planting it on page one and watching it grow.

So before you write your pilot, write your ending. Then sit back, open up ChatGPT, and say, "Okay, let's build the road back." You'll be amazed how fast and how clearly the story comes together when you know where it's all headed. That's not just a writing trick. That's the real secret behind every great show you've ever loved.

Why ChatGPT is Your Fastest Writing Partner

There's something thrilling about the blank page. It's full of promise, but it can also be paralyzing. That first word, that first scene, that first piece of dialogue—they all carry the weight of getting it right. And traditionally, writers have laboured over scripts for weeks, even months, afraid to make the wrong move. But now there's ChatGPT, and everything changes. Suddenly, you're not alone at the keyboard. You have a writing partner who never sleeps, never runs out of ideas, and never tells you your concept is too weird to work. In the world of screenwriting, ChatGPT is your shortcut to speed, clarity, and creative breakthroughs. It's the writing buddy who shows up 24/7 and never has a bad day.

Let's get something clear right away—ChatGPT isn't going to write your entire script for you unless you ask it to. And even then, it'll only be as good as what you feed it. The real magic happens when you use it like a partner, not a ghost-writer. It's like sitting across from someone who knows every trope, every story structure, every genre convention, and can suggest three different versions of a scene in less time than it takes to sip your coffee. This kind of speed means you can make decisions faster, test ideas instantly, and pivot without wasting hours down the wrong path. That's not just convenience—it's power.

Think about what usually slows down the writing process. You get stuck on character motivations, unsure how they would react. You can't figure out how to transition from one scene to the next. You know something's missing in the plot but can't quite put your finger on it. These are the moments where momentum dies. But with ChatGPT, you can pause, ask a question, and get ten possible answers in seconds. You don't need to walk away for a "break" or spiral into self-doubt. You just keep going. That's what makes it your fastest writing partner.

One of the smartest ways to use ChatGPT is for brainstorming. Let's say you have a vague idea—maybe a story about a con artist who poses as a grief counsellor. You can throw that at ChatGPT and say, "Give me ten pilot episode ideas for this premise." It will come back with several story outlines, character suggestions, emotional arcs, and conflict points you hadn't thought of. You're not starting from zero anymore. You're selecting from a menu of creative options, mixing and matching until something clicks. That speeds up your process before you've even written a word of the actual script.

ChatGPT also accelerates structural planning. Instead of spending hours trying to outline your three-act structure, you can describe your concept and ask ChatGPT to break it into acts. You can request scene breakdowns, cold open ideas, mid-act twists, or finale concepts. You can test multiple story rhythms to see which one feels best for your tone. The AI doesn't get attached to its answers, so you can keep trying until the outline clicks. And because it responds immediately, you're constantly moving forward instead of circling the same few beats.

Dialogue is another huge time sink for writers. It's hard to find the right voice for a character, especially early in the process. But you can have ChatGPT generate sample conversations between your characters. You don't even have to keep them—you just use them to get a feel for the rhythm, the personality, the tone. Maybe one line sparks something real. Maybe a whole scene falls into place. Either way, you're writing faster because you're not stuck staring at a blinking cursor, waiting for the right words to show up in your head.

Rewriting also becomes faster. Normally, you'd write a scene, feel unsure, let it sit, come back a day later, and maybe improve it. With ChatGPT, you can rewrite in real-time. Highlight the scene you don't love, explain what's not working, and let the AI pitch alternate versions. It's like having a built-in writer's room that never needs a lunch break.

You can even ask it to reframe scenes for a different emotional tone, shift character motivation, or push the pacing harder—and it'll give you options instantly.

Another speed boost comes from ChatGPT's ability to hold everything in context. As you work through your pilot, you can keep feeding it pieces of your script and ask for feedback or continuity suggestions. You can remind it of character arcs or themes you want to hit, and it'll help make sure those elements stay on track. This removes the need to constantly scroll back through your document, re-reading and re-checking every choice. You just ask, and it reminds you where everything fits.

Of course, the more specific you are, the better your results will be. ChatGPT is powerful, but it's not a mind reader. You have to know what you want out of the interaction. Are you looking for speed in plot generation, emotional impact, punchier dialogue, or just a smoother writing rhythm? The better your inputs, the sharper and more useful the responses. This book will help you get better at asking the right questions, framing your prompts, and steering the AI toward results that feel like they came from your own mind—but just faster.

Let's not pretend this is some magic wand. ChatGPT won't solve every writing problem instantly, and it won't stop you from needing to revise, rethink, or refine your ideas. But it will slash the time it takes to get from idea to finished draft. It will cut through the fog of indecision. It will help you make bold choices, try new approaches, and write like someone who doesn't have time for perfectionism. That's what makes it the fastest writing partner you've ever worked with.

If you want to write a pilot in one day, speed is everything—but it's only useful if you're writing the right things. ChatGPT helps you stay aligned with your core story, test options, and keep moving forward. It's not about rushing. It's about flow. And when you learn to write with that kind of creative momentum, suddenly the idea of banging out an entire TV pilot in a single focused day doesn't sound crazy. It sounds like fun.

So treat ChatGPT like a creative partner. Ask questions. Challenge its suggestions. Make bold decisions. And write like you've got a machine that can follow you anywhere your imagination leads.

Because now you do.

What Makes a Pilot Episode Unmissable?

If you ask anyone who works in television what the most important episode of a series is, they'll tell you without hesitation—it's the pilot. That first episode has to do a hundred things at once. It needs to introduce characters, establish tone, set up the world, tease long-term story arcs, deliver entertainment, and still leave the audience hungry for more. And it needs to do all of that in around 45 pages or less. That's a tall order. But when done right, a pilot becomes irresistible. It doesn't just start a story—it makes a promise. It invites the viewer into a world they don't want to leave. So what exactly makes a pilot episode unmissable?

It starts with clarity. The best pilots are confident. They know what the show is, what it isn't, and who it's for. They make decisions about tone, genre, pacing, and character right from the first scene. You don't get the sense that the writer is still trying to figure things out. You feel like you've stepped into something already living and breathing. That clarity makes people pay attention. When a pilot is tentative or vague, audiences drift. But when it feels like the show knows what it's doing and where it's going, viewers lock in.

Characters are the next major ingredient. Unmissable pilots introduce you to characters you either instantly love, want to understand, or can't stop watching because they're a glorious mess. These characters don't need to be likable in the traditional sense, but they must be compelling. They need to have something burning inside them—a desire, a fear, a flaw, or a mission. They need to feel real enough to root for or fear, and mysterious enough to keep you guessing. The more contradiction you can pack into their personalities without making them confusing, the more magnetic they become. And you need to introduce these characters quickly, clearly, and in situations that show us who they are, not just tell us.

Conflict is the fuel of a great pilot. There's no room for slow builds. A good pilot doesn't wait until the second episode to kick things off. Right away, something big needs to happen—or at least feel like it's about to. The status quo has to be broken. There has to be tension, both external and internal. Unmissable pilots often open with a bang, a mystery, or a decision that can't be undone. And that central conflict needs to be more than just plot—it has to reveal something about the characters and the world. That's where the emotional connection begins.

World-building is another massive part of the appeal. Even if the show takes place in a familiar setting like a high school or a city hospital, the world of the show has to feel specific. The rules, the relationships, the social dynamics—these things matter. And if your show lives in a more heightened world, like sci-fi, fantasy, or an alternate reality, you need to introduce those elements efficiently. Not by dumping exposition, but by letting the audience experience the world naturally through action and character. A great pilot gives just enough information to intrigue but not so much that it overwhelms. It respects the audience's intelligence and trusts them to keep up.

Theme gives your pilot depth. What is this show really about under the surface? Not just the plot, but the deeper message or question. Is it about justice? Redemption? Identity? Survival? Belonging? You don't need to spell it out, but the best pilots make the theme felt. It shows up in the choices characters make, in the setting, in the atmosphere, and in the way conflicts unfold. When a pilot has a strong theme, viewers sense that the story has something to say—and they want to hear it.

Another thing unmissable pilots do well is pacing. There's no wasted space. Every scene serves a function—revealing character, pushing the plot, or setting up future twists. There's a rhythm to the episode that keeps pulling you forward.

Even quieter scenes carry tension. Even humorous moments serve a deeper purpose. The pilot feels tight, like there's no fat on it. It's lean and hungry, and it keeps the audience in a state of anticipation.

Then there's the hook. That one moment that happens in the last minute, the last scene, or even the last line that makes people shout, "I need to see what happens next." It could be a shocking reveal, an unexpected twist, or just a powerful emotional beat that redefines everything we've just seen. That hook is your mic drop. It's the thing that transforms a good pilot into a great one. And often, it's the scene that gets a show picked up or passed over. You need to build your entire pilot with that moment in mind. The hook is what sends people straight to the next episode, or leaves them talking about your script long after they've put it down.

Now let's talk about how ChatGPT can help you make your pilot unmissable. Because the truth is, doing all of this on your own in one day is a major challenge. But with AI, you've got the support to explore options quickly, test ideas instantly, and tighten your script in real time. You can use ChatGPT to brainstorm multiple character introductions, rewrite your hook in ten different ways, adjust pacing scene by scene, or even generate thematic language to subtly reinforce your story's deeper message. You're no longer trapped in your own head. You're in a creative dialogue with a writing partner who can push you to find your best version of every moment.

You can also ask ChatGPT to analyze your pilot as you go. Feed it a scene and ask if the theme is coming through. Ask if the character feels consistent. Ask if the tension drops too much in the middle. These aren't things you'd normally be able to fix instantly. But now you can. You can move fast *and* write smart.

The goal here isn't just to write any pilot. It's to write one that makes people sit up, lean in, and forget they're reading a script. A pilot that feels alive from the first line to the last frame. One that opens a door and makes the audience desperate to see what's behind it. That's what makes a pilot episode unmissable—and now you have the tools and the method to write one in a single, focused day.

It's not about writing faster for the sake of speed. It's about writing better because you're using the momentum of real-time collaboration. So when you're working on your pilot, keep asking yourself: Am I grabbing attention? Am I revealing character? Am I raising questions? Am I making a promise that the rest of the show will want to keep? If the answer is yes, then congratulations—you're writing a pilot that no one will want to miss.

How to Turn a Tiny Idea into a TV Concept

Every TV show you've ever loved started with something small. A fragment. A spark. A character flaw. A situation. An overheard line in a coffee shop. What separates those tiny moments from the kind that get forgotten is how they're shaped into full concepts. A great idea doesn't just live in your head as a random what-if. It becomes a machine—a structure that can generate stories, characters, conflict, and longevity. And the key to transforming that tiny idea into a TV-ready concept is knowing how to stretch it, test it, flip it, and ask the right questions. And guess what? ChatGPT is designed to help you do all of that in real time.

Let's say you have the smallest seed of an idea: "A guy wakes up and realizes everyone in his town is gone." That's it. That's not a concept yet. But it's a doorway. You could ignore it or get stuck wondering if it's been done before. Or you could plug it into a creative process, break it open, and find out what lives inside it. Start by asking what genre it might fit. Is this a sci-fi thriller? A slow-burn horror? A quirky comedy? A drama about loneliness and isolation? The genre you choose gives you your tone, your stakes, your world rules. So throw that question to ChatGPT: "What are five different genre directions I could take with a story where a guy wakes up and his town is empty?" In seconds, you'll get options that reframe the idea in ways you probably hadn't considered.

The next step is character. Who is this guy? Why him? Why now? What makes his experience more interesting than if it happened to someone else? A tiny idea becomes a usable concept when it attaches to someone with depth. So start exploring his life. Is he someone who wanted everyone to go away? Is this his punishment, his wish come true, or the consequence of something he did? Ask ChatGPT to help build out a character profile. You'll get motivations, flaws, habits, even background storylines that start to suggest more and more episodes.

Then look at scale. A pilot is just the beginning. So when you're shaping a concept, you have to ask: can this idea generate stories over time? Can it grow into something bigger? A great TV concept isn't just about what happens—it's about what *keeps* happening. What's the mystery? What's the conflict that sustains more than one episode? ChatGPT is amazing at this. Try asking, "What ongoing mysteries or conflicts could stem from this idea?" or "How could this evolve into a multi-season arc?" That's when your one-sentence idea begins to stretch into a world. You start to see not just one story, but ten. Twenty. More.

A good TV concept also needs some kind of hook—something that makes people go, "That's different," or "I need to see that." It doesn't have to be loud, but it has to be sharp. Maybe your show is told in reverse order. Maybe each episode starts with a lie that gets revealed by the end. Maybe the main character dies at the end of season one and the show continues without them. These are concept-level choices that elevate the basic idea into something new. And again, ChatGPT can pitch those twists endlessly. You just keep iterating until one jumps out at you and says, "That's the one."

Tone is another layer that transforms an idea. Is your show funny? Cynical? Optimistic? Bleak? The same core idea can play wildly differently depending on tone. "A guy wakes up alone in his town" could become a dry, Wes Anderson-style comedy, or a paranoid, Christopher Nolan-style mind-bender. Ask ChatGPT to pitch you tonal variations, and you'll see just how many directions one idea can take. This is how you start to get control over your concept, because you're no longer guessing. You're choosing from a tailored list of options that match your creative instincts.

And don't forget about theme. Every great TV show, even the ones that seem silly or superficial, is actually about something deeper. Love, trust, survival, redemption, family, power, control—these ideas give emotional weight to the structure. So take your tiny idea and ask, "What could this show *really* be about?" You're not writing essays about it.

You're just using theme to steer the story. When you align your plot and your character arcs with a central theme, you get that magical feeling that everything belongs. ChatGPT can help unpack theme and even pitch stories that embody it, keeping you anchored while your idea grows.

One of the fastest ways to test if your idea is becoming a usable concept is to imagine a logline. Not a full synopsis, just a sentence that describes the setup, the character, and the central conflict or situation. If your idea can be shaped into a logline that makes someone lean forward, you're on the right track. And yes, ChatGPT is great at writing loglines. Ask it for ten, then tweak the one that comes closest to your vision. You can even ask it to generate variations for different genres or tones, helping you zero in on the best fit.

Once you have a solid logline, test the premise by imagining the first episode. If you can outline the pilot, you've got a concept. If you can outline five more episodes, you've got a series. Use ChatGPT to help build that out. Ask it for episode summaries. Ask it to expand on conflicts, recurring characters, long-term arcs. You'll be amazed how quickly a tiny thought you almost ignored turns into something that could anchor an entire season.

And here's the final trick—just keep playing. A tiny idea doesn't become a concept through pressure or perfectionism. It grows through exploration. The more questions you ask, the more creative prompts you throw at ChatGPT, the more you'll find yourself shaping something that feels unique, meaningful, and ready for the screen.

Ideas are everywhere. But concepts? Those are forged. And now you have the tools to do that in one creative burst. You don't need to spend weeks wondering if your idea is worth writing. You can test it, grow it, and outline it in hours. That's what ChatGPT allows you to do. So don't wait for inspiration to turn into something big on its own. Take the smallest spark, and start building. You're one good question away from your next great series.

Building a World the Audience Wants to Visit Again

Some shows work because of their characters, some because of the plot, but the ones that become cultural touchstones—the ones that people rewatch endlessly, write fan fiction about, and recommend with glowing eyes—are the ones that build unforgettable worlds. The setting isn't just a backdrop. It's a character in itself. Whether it's a quiet seaside town hiding dark secrets, a futuristic colony on Mars, a strange high school where weird things happen every week, or even the familiar setting of a Brooklyn apartment block, the world needs to pull the viewer in and make them want to stay. So how do you build a world that people want to keep coming back to? That's where your imagination—and ChatGPT—become a dream team.

It all starts with one simple question: what's different about this world? Even if your show is set in the real world, something has to set it apart. Maybe it's the subculture. Maybe it's the rules that govern behavior. Maybe it's the way people talk or the visual style or the sense of time. You're looking for that special sauce that makes your world feel fresh, even if it's familiar. The audience doesn't need to see flying cars or alien moons to feel transported. They just need to feel like this place, whatever it is, has its own identity. Ask ChatGPT to help brainstorm "what makes this world unique" and you'll get ideas that challenge your first instincts and open up new creative angles.

A great world has rules. What can happen here? What can't? Who has power? Who doesn't? What's considered normal in this place that wouldn't be normal anywhere else? These rules don't need to be spelled out in exposition. They can be shown through action, dialogue, and choices. But they do need to be consistent. That consistency creates trust between the audience and the story. If your world feels believable within its own logic, viewers will go along for the ride. And when you need help tightening or clarifying those rules, ChatGPT can help spot inconsistencies or even generate a codified "rulebook" for your world that you can reference as you write.

Another piece of the puzzle is geography. You don't need a full map, but you should know where things are and how people move through the world. Is the town laid out like a maze? Is the spaceship claustrophobic? Is the castle surrounded by a forest that everyone avoids? Locations are more than just places to stage scenes—they shape how characters live, how they interact, and what kind of stories are possible. When you're creating your locations, ask ChatGPT for descriptions, symbolic meaning, and even ways to use those places to reinforce character or theme. Suddenly, your main character's cluttered bookstore isn't just a job—it's a metaphor for their fear of letting go.

Then there's culture. What do people value here? What do they fear? What are the unspoken social rules? Is this a place of gossip and secrets? A place where appearances matter more than truth? A place where rebellion simmers beneath the surface? Culture gives your world texture. You can use it to create tension, comedy, or both. ChatGPT is incredibly helpful in generating social dynamics, belief systems, slang, rituals, even the kinds of restaurants, music, or traditions that define the world. You can ask for variations, mix and match, and see what resonates with the tone you're aiming for.

Let's talk about time. Some shows live in the now. Others feel timeless. Some are set in the near future or distant past. Time affects technology, language, fashion, and mindset. If your show is contemporary, how contemporary is it? Is it reacting to current issues? If it's historical, how true to history will you be? If it's futuristic, is it utopian, dystopian, or something in between? You can even play with time within the narrative—flashbacks, time loops, or stories that unfold across generations. Whatever you choose, make sure it serves the emotional arc of the characters. And if you're stuck trying to imagine what your world looks like in a specific time frame, just describe it to ChatGPT and ask it to generate rich, detailed imagery or cultural context.

Mood is another major ingredient. A world's emotional feel is just as important as its visual details. Is your world mysterious, melancholic, chaotic, dreamy, gritty, absurd? The atmosphere will bleed into everything—from dialogue to camera angles to musical choices. And it starts with your writing. ChatGPT can help you explore tone and emotion scene by scene. You can tell it to rewrite a setting description to feel more eerie, more hopeful, more oppressive—and it will. Use that power to shape the emotional texture of your world in a way that invites the audience into a specific experience, not just a physical place.

Now let's talk about re-watchability. What makes a world worth returning to isn't just surface-level coolness. It's layers. Subtext. Foreshadowing. Hidden meaning. Things the audience misses the first time and catches on the second or third viewing. Planting details early that pay off later is the hallmark of great world-building. So don't be afraid to hide secrets in plain sight. ChatGPT is great at helping you do this. You can ask for symbolism, double meanings, or "Easter eggs" that tie into later episodes. This kind of world-building builds trust and reward into the viewing experience, which makes people want to come back.

And of course, great world-building works best when it's tightly connected to character. The world should reflect the protagonist's journey. If your main character is dealing with abandonment, maybe the world is falling apart, or feels cold and impersonal. If they're coming of age, the world might be full of danger and wonder at the same time. Ask ChatGPT to help mirror your world to your character arc, and you'll create an experience that feels emotionally cohesive, not just visually cool.

A world that people want to visit again isn't necessarily the biggest or most elaborate. It's the one that feels alive. The one that reacts to the characters' choices. The one that makes the audience feel like there's always something just out of view, waiting to be discovered. With ChatGPT, you don't need months of solitary world-building. You can test ideas, deepen them, and bring them to life in minutes. You can walk through your world like a tour guide with a brilliant assistant constantly adding richness and depth behind the scenes.

So whether your story takes place on an alien planet, a 1980s arcade, a secret underground society, or a single small-town diner, your job is to make that place unforgettable. Give it detail. Give it conflict. Give it emotional weight. And most importantly, give it the kind of intrigue that keeps people wanting to return. Because once your audience falls in love with the world, they'll follow your story anywhere.

Crafting Characters That Walk Off the Page

A great pilot can have a killer premise, clever twists, and flawless structure, but none of it matters if the characters fall flat. The audience doesn't tune in week after week just to see what happens—they tune in to see *who* it happens to. That's why creating characters that feel real, unpredictable, and emotionally alive is the most important job you have as a screenwriter. Characters who walk off the page aren't just names in a script. They breathe. They ache. They contradict themselves. They have hopes, habits, secrets, and stories that don't all fit into the first episode. And when done right, they become the heart of your show.

So how do you create characters that feel so real that the audience starts thinking of them like old friends—or enemies? You start by thinking in layers. Surface traits are just the beginning. Yes, you can give your character a profession, a fashion sense, or a favorite drink, but that's not who they are. Who they are comes from what they want, what they fear, what they're hiding, and what they're willing to sacrifice. Those are the engines that drive them through the story. And those are the things ChatGPT can help you uncover faster than hours of staring at a character sheet.

Take a name—any name—and throw it into ChatGPT. Say, "Give me a character profile for someone named Jordan Ellis, a street magician in Las Vegas." In seconds, you'll get a backstory, a list of personality traits, maybe even a family history or flaw you hadn't considered. You can keep refining it by asking, "What does Jordan want more than anything?" or "What lie does Jordan tell themselves?" These questions aren't just for fun—they're the spine of your character's arc. The more you play with the answers, the more alive your character becomes.

Conflict is the key to character, and internal conflict is often more powerful than external. If your character says one thing and does another, the audience leans in. If they desperately want love but sabotage every relationship, they become interesting. If they crave power but fear the responsibility that comes with it, you've created tension that can sustain an entire season. ChatGPT can help you build these contradictions by suggesting opposing traits or giving examples of how a character might behave when they're pulled in two directions at once.

Another trick is to define your characters by the choices they make under pressure. Anyone can be calm and noble when things are going well. But who are they when everything falls apart? Do they run? Do they lash out? Do they try to save others or themselves? Crafting those moments early in your pilot shows the audience who they're really dealing with. If you're unsure how your character might behave in crisis, just ask ChatGPT, "How would Jordan Ellis react if his best friend betrayed him?" You'll get several options, and each one can lead to new story directions.

Relationships are where characters really come to life. No one exists in a vacuum, and your pilot should give a sense of how each main character relates to others in the world. Who do they protect? Who threatens them? Who brings out their worst impulses? The dynamics between characters create texture and momentum. Even if two characters aren't in a scene together yet, you should know how they feel about each other. Use ChatGPT to explore pairings. Say, "Describe the dynamic between Jordan Ellis and his older sister, a police detective who disapproves of his lifestyle." Boom—instant friction, emotion, and opportunities for drama.

Dialogue is another space where your characters either come alive or fall flat. The best dialogue doesn't just sound good—it sounds *like them*. Each character should have their own rhythm, vocabulary, and way of seeing the world. One might speak in clipped sentences. Another might ramble when nervous. One might never say what they really mean. One might always go for the joke. ChatGPT is great for testing these voices. You can feed it a character description and ask it to generate sample conversations. Then you refine, steal lines, or simply use the flow to find your own version of the character's voice.

But it's not just about how they speak—it's what they *don't* say. Silence, subtext, hesitation, and avoidance all reveal character. Maybe your character deflects serious topics with humor. Maybe they constantly change the subject when someone gets too close. These behaviors add realism and depth. If you're struggling to find those beats, ask ChatGPT, "What are subtle ways a character might avoid talking about their traumatic past?" The responses might surprise you—and inspire scenes that weren't in your outline.

Backstory is essential, but don't dump it all in the pilot. You want to hint at it, tease it, let it leak out through behavior, implication, and carefully chosen lines. Audiences don't need to know everything about a character to feel invested—they just need to sense there's more beneath the surface. With ChatGPT, you can build a whole hidden history for a character and then decide how and when to reveal it over time. That's the kind of storytelling that makes characters feel larger than life.

Visual description helps too. While TV is a visual medium, you only get a few lines in the script to describe someone's appearance or vibe. You want it to be evocative without being overdone. Instead of saying someone is "tall and handsome," you might say "he walks like he's used to being followed." That gives casting directors and readers a sense of personality, not just looks. ChatGPT can help you brainstorm these visual hooks—just ask for vivid, character-based descriptions and tweak until it feels right.

And don't forget growth. Characters who stay the same aren't interesting. They need to change, resist change, relapse, evolve, or self-destruct. Think about where your character begins and where you want them to end up—emotionally, morally, even physically. Your pilot is the beginning of that arc, so you want to introduce both who they are and who they *might become*. If you're not sure what arc fits your concept, you can ask ChatGPT, "What are possible character arcs for someone like Jordan Ellis over a season of TV?" Then pick the one that excites you most and write toward it.

At the end of the day, characters that walk off the page do so because they surprise you. They make choices you didn't expect but that make perfect sense in hindsight. They carry emotional weight. They break your heart and make you laugh in the same scene. They reveal something about human nature that makes us reflect on our own lives. With the right prompts and a little back-and-forth, ChatGPT becomes your mirror, your sparring partner, your wild-card thinker—and it helps you unlock characters that feel as real as anyone you know.

So when you're writing your pilot, don't just fill the page with dialogue and direction. Fill it with people. People who lie, people who hope, people who carry pain and pride and problems you can't solve in just one episode. Those are the characters that make audiences fall in love. Those are the ones they'll follow anywhere.

Choosing the Right Genre for Your Story

Choosing the right genre isn't just about picking a label to slap on your pilot. It's about defining the rules of the world you're building, setting expectations for your audience, and shaping the tone and structure of everything you write. The genre you choose influences how your characters behave, what kind of conflicts they face, and how the story unfolds. It's the lens through which everything is filtered. And the truth is, the same basic idea can look wildly different depending on the genre you frame it in. That's why it's not just a box you check—it's a decision that defines your series at every level.

Let's say your core idea is about someone discovering a hidden truth about their identity. That could easily be a drama, a thriller, a comedy, or even a supernatural horror show. The plot beats might stay similar, but the mood, style, and emotional resonance would shift dramatically. In a drama, it might be an emotional journey of self-acceptance. In a thriller, it might lead to danger and paranoia. In a comedy, it could result in a series of hilarious misunderstandings. And in horror, that hidden truth might be something terrifying and inescapable. The genre choice is what brings that idea to life in a specific, visceral way.

If you're unsure what genre fits your idea best, ChatGPT is an incredible tool for helping you test out different approaches. You can say, "Here's my premise—show me how it would work in five different genres." ChatGPT will generate outlines, tone shifts, and character adjustments that make each version feel distinct. Suddenly, you're not guessing. You're exploring possibilities. This gives you the power to make a smart choice based on what excites you most—and what best serves the story you want to tell.

Genre also determines how much creative freedom you have with certain elements. If you're writing a grounded drama, there are limits to what feels believable. If you're writing science fiction or fantasy, the boundaries are more flexible, but the world-building becomes more demanding. A procedural crime show comes with structural expectations: a case to solve, a method to follow, a resolution by the end. A character-driven comedy can meander more and play with tone. Knowing your genre lets you lean into the strengths of that format instead of fighting against them.

It also helps you make consistent creative choices. Let's say you're writing a mystery. That genre thrives on tension, secrets, red herrings, and a slow reveal of truth. So if you suddenly throw in a slapstick scene or a romantic musical number, you risk breaking the tone unless that kind of tonal shift is part of your show's DNA. With genre clarity, you know what fits and what doesn't. And ChatGPT can help you pressure test those boundaries. You can ask, "Would this moment still work if I'm writing this as a noir mystery?" and get feedback instantly.

Audience expectation is another huge part of genre selection. People come to certain genres looking for specific experiences. If they start watching what they think is a comedy and it turns into a bleak tragedy halfway through the pilot, they're likely to feel confused or misled. But if you establish your genre clearly, you give the audience a kind of contract. They know what kind of emotional journey they're in for. They trust you. And once that trust is there, you can start playing with and even subverting expectations. But it all starts with clarity.

There's also the question of marketability. While you never want to write something just to chase trends, it's useful to be aware of what genres are selling and where your show might fit in the current landscape. If you're pitching to a streaming platform that's investing heavily in sci-fi or young adult drama, you want to know how your concept fits—or stands out—in that space. ChatGPT can help you research trends, compare your concept to existing shows, and even generate potential pitch angles tailored to a specific market.

But beyond trends and structure and tone, the most important reason to choose the right genre is that it gives your creativity a container. Not a cage, but a framework. Genre provides the ingredients you'll be working with: suspense, laughter, fear, romance, wonder. It's your toolkit. And the clearer you are about what kind of story you're telling, the more confidently you can build it.

If you're writing with ChatGPT, try asking it to reframe your pilot idea in a few different genres. Watch how the stakes shift, how the character dynamics change, how the plot finds new shapes. You might discover a version that feels far more alive than the one you originally had in mind. Or you might confirm that your first instinct was the right one. Either way, you'll be making that choice from a place of strength.

And remember, hybrid genres are a thing. Some of the most successful shows blend tones—dramedies, horror comedies, sci-fi thrillers. The trick is to blend them intentionally. Know which genre is driving the bus and which one is adding flavor. If the audience knows how to emotionally engage with your show, you can mix genres without losing them. ChatGPT can help you balance this. You can ask it to generate genre combinations, scene examples, or tonal transitions that help you blend without confusion.

In the end, genre is more than a label—it's your creative identity. It's what tells your audience, "This is the kind of story you're about to experience." And when that promise is clear and confidently delivered, the audience leans in. They know what they've signed up for, and they're ready to take the ride.

So don't rush the decision. Play. Explore. Use ChatGPT to twist your premise until it lands somewhere exciting. And when you choose your genre, commit to it. Let it shape your world, your characters, your pace, your tone. Because when you get that right, everything else falls into place.

Generating Plot with ChatGPT in Real-Time

The idea of plotting a TV pilot used to be this slow, lonely grind of sticky notes, index cards, and hours of second-guessing every decision. You'd brainstorm, then re-brainstorm, only to hit a wall halfway through the second act because something felt off and you weren't sure what. It was like building a house without blueprints—hoping it would all hold up in the end. But now, writing doesn't have to work like that. With ChatGPT, generating plot in real-time becomes this thrilling back-and-forth—like having a writer's room on speed dial. You're no longer waiting for inspiration to strike. You're in constant motion, feeding the machine your vision and watching it evolve right in front of you.

Let's say you've got a rough idea for your pilot: it's about a social worker in a small town who discovers that the town's darkest secrets are being hidden in plain sight. That's a nice setup, but what happens next? What scenes will fill out the episode? How does it end? That's where most writers start spinning their wheels. But with ChatGPT, you don't have to stew. You simply type in, "Break down a 3-act pilot episode based on this idea," and within seconds, you're staring at a complete skeleton. It's not set in stone, but it's something solid to react to. And that's the point—it's always easier to shape something than to build from nothing.

Real-time plot generation isn't about letting the AI take over the story. It's about using it to stretch your imagination, stress test your instincts, and fill in the spaces your brain hasn't reached yet. You might have the first act nailed down and need help with the midpoint twist. Or maybe you've written a great ending but don't know how to build to it naturally. ChatGPT lets you laser in on those gaps. You can say, "Give me three plot turns that would raise the stakes in the middle of this story," or "Suggest a complication that forces my protagonist to make a hard choice." Boom. New ideas, instantly. Now you can pick what works, remix what doesn't, and keep moving forward without losing momentum.

One of the coolest ways to work is to generate your scenes one at a time while talking to ChatGPT like a co-writer. Start with your opening scene. Feed it a few lines of setup. Ask, "What would logically happen next?" or "What's an unexpected twist that still fits the tone?" And just like that, you're collaborating. As each scene unfolds, you can make choices, refine the flow, and build tension—all in real time. You don't have to shut your creative flow down to think through structure. You're doing both at once: writing and plotting in sync.

You can also build out character-driven plots by focusing on motivation. Say your main character has a secret addiction. That's a great internal conflict, but how does it affect the external plot? Ask ChatGPT, "How could my character's addiction lead to a crisis in act two?" or "How might this secret get revealed at the worst possible time?" The AI will give you multiple directions that keep your character arc tied directly to the story beats. And that connection is what separates an okay plot from a great one—it's all about cause and effect rooted in emotional truth.

Real-time plotting is also ideal for making your pilot episode feel like a complete story while still launching a series. That's a tough balance to strike. You want closure on the episode's arc, but you also need to plant seeds for future episodes. You can ask ChatGPT, "What's a satisfying way to end the pilot that still leaves big questions unanswered?" or "What cliffhanger would make the audience desperate to watch episode two?" The suggestions you get can spark scenes that weren't even on your radar. And you'll know right away if they fit, because you're in the flow—you're writing them as you go.

You can even treat ChatGPT like a live note taker in your writing process. As you generate your scenes and ideas, you can paste everything into one conversation and periodically ask it to summarize or re-outline the episode based on what's been created so far. This is a lifesaver when you're deep into writing and lose track of your own structure. It keeps the whole plot clear and organized, letting you focus on emotional beats and character dynamics without scrambling to remember where you're headed.

Another great trick is generating alternate paths. Say you're stuck between two major decisions. Should your character stay in town or run away? Should they confront their enemy or protect them? Instead of agonizing over it for hours, throw the question to ChatGPT. Ask it to play out both options and show you the consequences of each one. You'll often find that one path has more tension, more conflict, or more emotional weight—and now you're not guessing. You've seen both roads. You're picking the one that's most effective.

And let's not forget the genre factor. If you're writing a thriller, you'll want suspense and twists baked into every act. If you're doing a comedy, the plot still needs structure but the beats will serve setups and punchlines. ChatGPT understands these nuances and can help shape your plot accordingly. Just say, "Plot this as a dark comedy instead of a straight drama," and you'll get tonal adjustments that keep the core story but change how it plays. This lets you test variations without rewriting everything from scratch.

There's a real joy in this kind of collaborative writing. It's fast, yes—but more importantly, it's energizing. You're not hitting a wall every time you face a blank section. You're not wondering what should happen next—you're asking. And getting answers. Instantly. Then adjusting, refining, and moving on. It becomes a rhythm. And once you find that rhythm, the pilot practically writes itself.

So if you're sitting there with a rough idea and no clear plan, don't wait for the whole story to magically appear in your head. Fire up ChatGPT. Start generating. Talk it out, scene by scene, question by question, beat by beat. Plot your pilot like you're in a room with the fastest brainstorming partner you've ever had. Because now you are. And suddenly, generating plot in real-time doesn't just feel possible—it feels inevitable.

Writing the Cold Open That Hooks Everyone

The cold open is your show's handshake. It's the moment that either invites the audience into your world or leaves them reaching for the remote. It's not just the beginning—it's the spark. In a matter of seconds, you need to grab attention, create intrigue, hint at what's to come, and make a promise that watching the next 40 minutes will be absolutely worth it. That's a big ask. And yet, the cold open doesn't have to explain everything—it just has to *hook*. When you write it right, it becomes unforgettable. And with ChatGPT in your corner, you can keep sharpening that moment until it hits like lightning.

A great cold open does one of three things: it shocks, it intrigues, or it immediately builds emotional connection. Sometimes, it does all three. It might start with a mysterious death, an awkward encounter, a huge explosion, a life-changing confession, or a completely mundane scene that spirals into chaos. The trick is to make the audience lean forward. They need to be thinking, *Wait, what's going on? Who are these people? What's going to happen next?* If your opening doesn't invite questions or create tension, you're giving your viewers permission to check out.

Let's look at some examples. The pilot of *Breaking Bad* opens with Walter White in his tighty-whities, crashing an RV in the desert, holding a gun, talking into a camcorder about his impending death. You don't know who he is or why he's doing this, but you're glued to the screen. It's strange. It's funny. It's tense. You *need* to know how he ended up there. Now contrast that with the cold open of *The Office*, where we simply meet the world's most awkward boss giving a terrible fake firing to his assistant. It's quiet, but hilarious and perfectly sets the tone. Same function, totally different energy. The genre and tone determine the kind of hook you need.

When you're writing your own cold open, you want to think about the emotional reaction you want from the audience. Do you want them shocked? Curious? Laughing? Heartbroken? Scared? Then build a short sequence that delivers that feeling in under three minutes. ChatGPT can help you generate several versions of the same opening with different emotional tones. For example, if your show is about a woman who fakes her death to escape her family, you could ask ChatGPT for cold opens that are dramatic, comedic, or suspenseful. Then you choose the one that hits the vibe you want.

One powerful strategy is to start *in media res*—in the middle of the action. Drop us into a moment with no setup. Something strange or high-stakes is already happening, and we're trying to catch up. This creates instant momentum. You can always flash back later to fill in the blanks, but in the cold open, mystery is your ally. Ask ChatGPT to help build an in media res moment around your story concept. You might get something wild you hadn't even considered—like a character fleeing a building in flames, or waking up in someone else's body, or standing at the altar with no idea who the groom is.

Another method is starting small and ending big. Begin with a seemingly ordinary moment—a morning routine, a casual conversation, a quiet setting—and then twist it at the last second. A knock at the door. A strange phone call. A detail in the background that doesn't belong. This kind of opening builds suspense through contrast. It draws the viewer in by making them feel safe, then turns that comfort into discomfort. Ask ChatGPT for a list of ways to subvert a quiet scene, and you'll be flooded with hooks that turn the mundane into the unforgettable.

Character is also key. If you're not leading with plot, you better lead with personality. Give us a moment that shows who this person is—flaws, strengths, quirks, contradictions. Maybe they're giving a speech they don't believe in. Maybe they're lying to their kids while planning a heist. Maybe they're singing karaoke alone in their car like it's a concert. These kinds of moments stick with people because they introduce someone we want to know more about. Ask ChatGPT to help craft an opening scene that introduces your main character in a unique or revealing way. The AI can help you shape that character moment until it feels specific, lived-in, and cinematic.

Dialogue in the cold open should be sharp, tight, and revealing. There's no room for fluff. Every line either deepens the mystery, sets the tone, or gives a clue. If you're struggling with the rhythm of your scene, use ChatGPT to workshop lines. You can feed it a sample and say, "Make this ten percent funnier," or "What's a stronger first line of dialogue here?" It can help you punch up the moment without killing the pacing.

You also want to consider visual elements. Even though you're writing a script, television is a visual medium. Your cold open should be written in a way that invites vivid imagery. What are we seeing that we haven't seen before? What's the visual that sticks in the viewer's mind? A woman standing ankle-deep in a frozen lake with a hammer in her hand. A man tied to a chair laughing hysterically at a romantic comedy playing on a tiny TV. Ask ChatGPT to help generate striking visual moments, and you'll never be short on ideas that grab attention.

And let's not forget music and sound. Even though you're not composing the soundtrack yourself, suggesting the tone can help shape the scene. Is there a song playing? Is there silence that makes everything feel tenser? Is there a radio broadcast in the background that delivers a key piece of exposition without anyone saying a word? These are the details that elevate your cold open and make it immersive. You can ask ChatGPT for ideas like, "Suggest a song or background sound that adds tension to this scene," and it'll offer mood-matching suggestions that enhance the moment.

Finally, remember that your cold open doesn't need to explain everything—it just needs to *promise* something. That promise might be emotional depth, nonstop action, layered mystery, or brilliant comedy. But the point is to leave the viewer with a sense of curiosity and anticipation. They need to feel like you've opened a door and they *have* to walk through it.

When you're working with ChatGPT, you're not guessing your way through a cold open. You're testing options in real time. You're saying, "Let's try it like this," and watching what changes. You're building until it clicks. You're finding that line, that image, that twist that makes someone go, "Oh yeah—I'm watching this." So take the pressure off yourself to write the perfect opening in one go. Let ChatGPT help you generate, revise, punch up, and reshape. Try different angles. Different tones. Different payoffs. Then choose the one that makes you excited to write the rest. Because if your cold open hooks you, chances are it'll hook everyone else too.

The First Ten Pages: Grabbing the Reader or Viewer

There's a kind of myth around the first ten pages of a TV pilot. Everyone talks about them like they're sacred, and honestly, they kind of are. If you can win someone over in those first ten, the rest of your script has a real shot. But if you don't grab them quickly, it doesn't matter how brilliant your third act twist is—no one's sticking around for it. Whether it's an exec, a producer, a script reader, or a bored viewer binge-scrolling late at night, you've got about ten pages to make them care. The good news is that these ten pages don't have to do everything—they just need to do the *right* things. And with ChatGPT in your corner, you can fine-tune those pages until they hum with energy, character, and potential.

Let's be real—when someone reads or watches your pilot, they're looking for a reason to stop. Not because they're cruel, but because they've seen too many scripts that go nowhere. They're scanning for signs that you know what you're doing, that your story is going somewhere, and that your characters are worth investing in. That's why your first ten pages have to work like an engine. They've got to fire on all cylinders—tone, character, conflict, intrigue. These aren't just setup pages. These are your *audition* pages.

One of the biggest mistakes writers make is thinking the first ten pages are just a prologue. A soft entry point. Some world-building, maybe a quirky introduction or two. But the truth is, the plot should already be moving. The stakes should already be rising. And the characters should already be making decisions. By page ten, your reader or viewer should know what kind of ride they're on, and why it matters. You don't need to explain everything, but you do need to show *something* compelling. That something can be a dilemma, a mystery, a power shift, or even just a killer line of dialogue that makes the reader sit up and say, "Okay, this writer's got something."

So what should be happening by page ten? Ideally, we've met the protagonist and seen them do something that reveals who they are—not just what they do. We've felt the tone of the show settle into place, whether it's gritty, whimsical, dark, hilarious, or totally weird. We've glimpsed the world, enough to get our bearings. And most importantly, we've been given a reason to lean in. A question, a choice, a threat, a promise—something that demands a response. If you can deliver that, you've done your job.

Let's say you're writing a political thriller. Your first ten pages might introduce us to the main character giving a public speech while simultaneously covering up a personal scandal. There's tension in the duality. We see public image vs. private truth. We sense that something's about to break. Now we want to know what it is and how this character's going to handle it. That's all it takes—one layered scene with stakes, tone, and personality.

Or maybe you're doing a coming-of-age dramedy. Your character is late for school, dodging their overly affectionate parent, getting detention for mouthing off, and all the while texting someone they're scared to meet in real life. Boom—we've got energy, emotion, and conflict. It doesn't need to be explosive. It just needs to feel alive.

Now here's where ChatGPT becomes your secret weapon. You can use it to test these first ten pages before you lock anything down. Feed in your concept and say, "Generate the first ten pages of a pilot that introduces this protagonist and sets up the main conflict." You'll get a solid draft—not a finished scene, but a real shape. Then you can pick it apart, rewrite, and fine-tune. Or you can say, "Here's my scene. How can I raise the stakes?" or "What's a sharper way to introduce this character's flaw?" ChatGPT will throw out ideas you hadn't considered—some you'll ignore, and some will be gold.

Another smart move is to ask ChatGPT to break your ten pages into beats. Scene by scene, line by line, what's happening? What's changing? Is the tension rising? Are the characters growing clearer? If the beats are flat or redundant, you'll see it immediately. Then you can adjust. Speed things up. Cut what doesn't move the story. Add sharper turns. Writing with momentum is the key, and ChatGPT helps keep you moving forward instead of circling the same slow start.

And don't underestimate the power of dialogue in these first pages. Great dialogue tells us who the characters are without spelling it out. It reveals relationship dynamics. It plays with subtext. If your opening scene is just people exchanging information, you're wasting precious space. Use ChatGPT to workshop banter, create tension, or add humor. Say, "Rewrite this conversation to feel more hostile under the surface," and you'll be surprised how much sharper your characters can sound.

Visuals matter, too. Even though you're writing for television and not a novel, the reader still needs to *see* the world. What are the sights, sounds, details that make this place feel specific? A weird piece of graffiti. A broken vending machine. A dog that always barks at 7 a.m. These aren't just flavor—they're the signs of a lived-in world. You can ask ChatGPT to generate location descriptions or sensory details that heighten the scene's texture. It keeps things grounded and immersive.

Lastly, don't forget to end those ten pages with a punch. Not necessarily a cliffhanger, but a shift. Something should change by the time we hit page ten. A question is asked. A secret is revealed. A plan is set in motion. This doesn't have to be huge—it just has to matter. Ask ChatGPT to suggest ten story beats that would make a great page ten moment, and you'll get a buffet of ideas to try. Pick the one that stings. That sticks.

At the end of the day, the first ten pages aren't about showing off. They're about making someone feel something. Curiosity. Tension. Excitement. Laughter. Fear. Give them a reason to keep going. Use ChatGPT like a creative pressure cooker—generate, refine, experiment, and distill. When those pages start clicking, you'll know. Because suddenly, you won't be asking *if* someone will keep reading. You'll be asking *how fast* they're going to want episode two.

Designing the Main Conflict in the Series

If your characters are the heart of your TV series, then conflict is the blood pumping through every scene. It's what drives the story forward, what gives your characters purpose, what keeps the audience on edge and emotionally invested. Without conflict, even the best dialogue, most imaginative world, and most charismatic characters fall flat. So when you're writing your pilot, you're not just writing a one-off story—you're laying the foundation for the main conflict that will fuel the entire series. And with ChatGPT by your side, designing this long-term conflict becomes a focused, dynamic, and even exciting part of the process.

Let's start by getting something straight: your pilot doesn't need to *resolve* the main conflict. It just needs to *ignite* it. You're creating the spark that sets off the chain reaction. That spark might be an event, a discovery, a betrayal, or a realization. Whatever it is, it should challenge your protagonist in a way that cannot be easily solved or ignored. The main conflict has to be big enough, sticky enough, and emotionally resonant enough to carry the weight of multiple episodes—if not multiple seasons.

So how do you figure out what your show's central conflict really is? Start by asking, "What does my protagonist want, and what's stopping them from getting it?" That's your story engine. The answer could be personal, political, emotional, moral, or even metaphysical. A detective wants justice but is haunted by their past. A teenager wants freedom but is stuck in a rigid religious community. A scientist wants to save the planet but is being silenced by the very corporation funding their work. These aren't just situational problems—they're life-defining struggles. That's the kind of conflict that builds a series.

You can use ChatGPT to refine this. Start by typing out your character's core desire, then ask, "What are five major obstacles that could block this character from achieving that goal over a long arc?" ChatGPT will give you enemies, dilemmas, environments, and even psychological barriers that help you flesh out the opposition. Then ask, "Which of these conflicts would evolve naturally over multiple episodes?" Now you're thinking like a showrunner, not just a writer.

Another powerful way to think about conflict is on three levels: internal, interpersonal, and external. The internal conflict is what your protagonist struggles with inside themselves—fear, guilt, trauma, identity. The interpersonal conflict is the tension between characters—alliances, betrayals, rivalries, misunderstandings. The external conflict is what's happening in the world—wars, systems, secrets, disasters. The most compelling TV series usually weave all three together. ChatGPT can help you brainstorm these levels by asking, "What's an internal struggle that mirrors this external situation?" or "How could this relationship add tension to the character's larger goal?"

Let's say your show is about a whistle-blower in a biotech company. The external conflict is clear: the company is hiding dangerous experiments. But that's not enough. You add interpersonal conflict: the whistle-blower's mentor is involved, and outing the company means destroying someone they care about. Then layer in internal conflict: they've always been afraid of confrontation and now must risk everything. Now you're not just telling a story about corruption—you're telling a story about bravery, loyalty, identity, and consequence. That's what makes the conflict feel rich and sustaining.

Pacing also matters. A good series conflict has layers that peel back gradually. You don't reveal the whole game in episode one. You hint. You mislead. You show glimpses of the bigger picture. Each episode should add complexity, deepen stakes, or flip something on its head. This is how the conflict evolves instead of feeling repetitive. Ask ChatGPT to help you map out the evolution. Try, "How can this conflict expand in season one without resolving?" or "What reveals could raise the stakes every three episodes?" This kind of long-view plotting is where AI can really accelerate your process.

Another smart tactic is building your main conflict around a moral dilemma. The best conflicts don't just ask, "Will they win?" They ask, "What will it cost them?" Give your protagonist a reason to hesitate. Maybe achieving their goal would mean hurting someone they love. Maybe they have to compromise their principles to win. ChatGPT can help you shape these dilemmas into scenes, arguments, and character beats. You can say, "Create a scenario where the character must choose between their mission and their morality," and watch how it plays out.

Don't forget the antagonist. The main conflict is often personified by someone—or something—that pushes against the protagonist at every turn. This doesn't have to be a villain in the classic sense. It can be a system, a belief, a force of nature, or even a version of the protagonist themselves. But if you *do* have an antagonist, make them strong, complex, and believable. ChatGPT can help you sketch them out: "Describe an antagonist who believes they're the hero in this conflict," or "What personal stake could the antagonist have in this battle?" The richer they are, the richer the conflict becomes.

The last thing to remember is that your main conflict doesn't have to be static. It should grow. It should mutate. Sometimes, halfway through a season, you realize the conflict isn't what you—or the protagonist—thought it was. That kind of shift re-energizes the series. Use ChatGPT to brainstorm reveals and reversals that keep the pressure on and the story moving. Ask, "What truth could change how the protagonist sees everything?" or "What if the antagonist was right all along?"

Designing the main conflict of your series isn't about creating one big problem to solve—it's about creating an engine that keeps generating new problems, new questions, new angles. It's the difference between a one-shot story and a living, breathing world. With ChatGPT helping you throw ideas at the wall, test them, reshape them, and organize them, you can build a conflict that not only launches your pilot—but sustains a whole universe of episodes waiting to be written.

How to Introduce Your Protagonist with Style

There's a special kind of magic that happens when a protagonist enters a scene for the first time and instantly grabs the audience's attention. It's not about dramatic entrances or flashy monologues—although those can work. It's about presence. It's about saying, without saying, *this is the person you're going to follow, love, question, root for, or fear.* Introducing your protagonist is one of the most important moments in your pilot, and how you do it sets the tone not just for the episode, but for the entire series. The audience doesn't need a backstory dump or a résumé—they need a *moment.* And if that moment is done right, they'll be hooked. Fortunately, with a tool like ChatGPT, you can shape that moment with layers, texture, and cinematic flair.

The first thing to keep in mind is that your protagonist is a moving target. Who they are in the beginning is not who they'll be by the end of the season, or even the end of the pilot. But the way you introduce them should reveal the core of their conflict, their flaw, or the world they live in. That introduction is your chance to define their energy. Are they in control or barely holding it together? Do they command the room or hide in the corner? Are they funny, intense, broken, brilliant? These choices speak louder than exposition ever could.

A great protagonist introduction usually does three things: it shows the character in action, it reveals their personality through behavior—not dialogue—and it raises a question. That question might be, "Why are they doing that?" or "What happened to make them this way?" or "Can they keep this up?" Those questions are gold. They build investment. They make the audience lean forward, wanting to know more. You don't need to spell everything out. In fact, it's better if you don't.

Let's take a look at some examples. In *Mad Men*, we meet Don Draper trying to sell cigarettes while casually flirting and researching what makes smokers tick. He's confident, smooth, clearly carrying some secrets. He's not introduced with narration or backstory—he's introduced by doing what he does best: manipulating truth. That's not just his job—it's who he is. In *Killing Eve*, we meet Villanelle smiling at a child, then knocking over her ice cream as she walks out. It's funny, unsettling, and it says everything about her in one simple, surprising beat.

When it comes to writing your own introduction, think about where your character is emotionally. What's their normal? What do they believe about themselves or the world that's about to be challenged? Now drop them into a situation that either reinforces or cracks that belief. Maybe your protagonist thinks they're in control—but the opening shows the first crack. Maybe they think they're invisible—and someone sees them in a way no one else has. You can use ChatGPT to brainstorm scenarios that reflect your character's core belief. Just say, "Give me an opening scene where my character feels like a fraud but has to pretend they're an expert," and you'll get story-driven intros full of conflict and depth.

Another trick is to introduce your protagonist *through contrast.* Put them in a room where everyone else is different. Their energy should either disrupt the space or feel completely out of sync with it. A nun walking into a biker bar. A tech genius at a nature retreat. A soldier at a kindergarten party. That tension between who they are and where they are immediately creates curiosity. You can ask ChatGPT to pitch scenes that reveal a character through contrast, and it'll throw you a range of tonal and situational ideas to play with.

Don't forget the visual cues. While you only get a few lines in a script to describe what someone looks like, those lines matter. You don't need to describe hair color or body type—you need to convey vibe. Is the character dressed like they don't care, or like they care too much? Are they composed, or do they carry the kind of nervous energy that makes everyone else uneasy? One powerful image can do more than a paragraph of explanation. ChatGPT can help you craft those descriptions with a few inputs. Say, "Describe a protagonist who hides their anxiety behind a carefully curated fashion style," and you'll get fresh, specific imagery to plug into your scene.

Dialogue can also be a sharp tool for introductions, but it has to be character-driven. Don't use it to explain who they are—use it to show *how* they interact. Are they defensive? Charming? Overly honest? Do they talk too much or say very little? A great first line of dialogue can become iconic because it reflects something true and unique about the character's voice. You can give ChatGPT a character description and ask, "What's a killer first line this person might say?" The more specific your character input, the better the results.

Relationships can also help define a character fast. Maybe you introduce your protagonist through a conversation with someone who either challenges them or enables them. Who people are around others tells us who they are. Show them protecting someone, lying to someone, deflecting with humor, or trying too hard to impress. That small interaction gives the audience a way in. You can ask ChatGPT, "Create an opening scene where my protagonist is pretending to care during a conversation with their partner," and use that to shape both tone and character dynamic.

What you want, ultimately, is for your audience to feel like they've *met* your protagonist—not just seen them. By the end of their first scene, we should feel something—maybe respect, maybe suspicion, maybe sympathy—but we should *feel.* If you're unsure if the introduction is landing, use ChatGPT to run a character audit. Paste in your scene and ask, "Based on this intro, what does this character seem to be like?" If the analysis doesn't match what you intended, you can rework the beats to align more closely with your vision.

And here's one more thing to keep in mind: the way you introduce your protagonist should hint at who they might become. Maybe not clearly, maybe not directly—but the seeds of the arc should be there. If they're going to evolve, fall, grow, or transform, let the first scene hold a little echo of that. Ask ChatGPT, "How can this scene suggest that this character might change by the end of the season?" and refine accordingly.

You don't get a second chance to introduce your lead. That moment is precious. It sets the tone, builds the connection, and opens the door for everything that follows. So make it count. Let your character walk onto the page or screen with style—not because they're flashy or loud, but because they're *true.* They feel like someone we've never met, but want to know everything about. And that's when the magic begins.

Creating the Supporting Cast That Completes the World

A TV show doesn't live or die by its protagonist alone. In fact, some of the most memorable moments in television history didn't even involve the main character—they happened between side characters, unexpected duos, or the wildcard that walked in halfway through the series and stole every scene. A strong supporting cast doesn't just orbit the lead—they enrich the world, shape the emotional landscape, and often carry entire storylines of their own. If your protagonist is the lens through which we view your story, your supporting characters are the texture that fills out the frame. They bring contrast, conflict, comfort, and color. Without them, the world feels thin. With them, it becomes alive. And with ChatGPT in your creative toolkit, you can develop a fully fleshed-out ensemble that breathes alongside your lead character.

When thinking about your supporting cast, the first instinct is usually to assign roles—best friend, love interest, antagonist, comic relief. That's a fine place to start, but it's not where you should stop. If each character exists solely to support or serve the main character's journey, the audience will feel it. You want characters who have their own goals, flaws, secrets, and arcs—even if those arcs are smaller. The best supporting characters don't just respond to the plot—they push it. They add tension, challenge the protagonist, enable them, betray them, or reflect them in unexpected ways.

One of the smartest ways to approach the supporting cast is to start with your protagonist. Ask, "What parts of my lead character's personality are missing, hidden, or in conflict?" Then build characters who either expose those parts or bring out the opposite. If your protagonist is tightly wound and afraid of failure, maybe they're paired with someone reckless and impulsive. If they're emotionally closed off, maybe a relentlessly honest character keeps cracking through the surface. These dynamics create friction and comedy, and more importantly, they reveal who your main character really is. You can ask ChatGPT to help brainstorm contrasting personalities that would naturally challenge your protagonist and spark interesting moments.

Another great angle is to mirror. Supporting characters can also be a distorted reflection of the lead—someone who made a different choice at a similar crossroads. This character becomes a kind of "what if" or even a warning. If your protagonist is a cop trying to stay clean, the mirrored character could be a former partner who sold out and climbed the ranks. The emotional charge of those parallels gives depth to both characters. You can use ChatGPT to explore these mirrors by saying, "Create a supporting character who is a reflection of my lead but with a darker philosophy," and you'll get compelling options you can shape and personalize.

You also want to consider relationships beyond how they relate to the main character. Do your supporting characters have history with each other? Inside jokes? Resentments? Romantic tension? Power struggles? These connections make the world feel bigger than one person's story. In ensemble shows like *The Wire* or *Orange Is the New Black*, the web of relationships becomes as important as the protagonist. Ask ChatGPT to help map out connections between your characters—who likes who, who hates who, who's secretly working together—and suddenly, your cast becomes a world within itself.

Diversity in personality, background, voice, and purpose is key. Not every character should be snarky, not every character should be brooding, and not every character should talk the same way. Think about different energies. A sarcastic realist, an anxious optimist, a deadpan outsider, a warm-hearted schemer. These contrasting voices add music to your dialogue and make each scene more dynamic. You can ask ChatGPT to generate profiles for a variety of character types and then mix and match until your cast starts to feel like a real group of individuals instead of placeholders.

And let's not forget function. Each supporting character should have a job in the story—even if it's subtle. Maybe one provides exposition in a way that feels natural. Another gives the audience access to an emotional side of the lead that no one else sees. One character might act as the devil on the protagonist's shoulder, urging them to take shortcuts, while another is the moral compass. These roles don't need to be rigid, but they help you keep your story on track. ChatGPT can help with this too—ask it, "What role could this character play in the plot's development?" or "How might this supporting character be used to raise the stakes in episode four?"

You also want to think long-term. Can this character grow? Can they surprise us? The best supporting characters evolve, just like the protagonist. They get their own arcs—maybe smaller, maybe slower, but still meaningful. Ask yourself where you want each of them to be by the end of the season. Even if the audience doesn't see that full journey in the pilot, planting the seeds early makes them more engaging. Use ChatGPT to sketch out mini-arcs—"Give me a five-episode emotional journey for this supporting character"—and see how that growth might ripple into the main story.

And finally, supporting characters are a great space for tone. Want to add levity without undercutting drama? That's a character. Want to explore darker themes without putting the weight solely on the lead? That's another character. You can stretch your world's emotional range through the supporting cast. The goofy best friend. The nihilistic sibling. The eccentric neighbor who stumbles into serious wisdom. These characters give you range without having to shift your protagonist's core identity. You can use ChatGPT to generate tonally contrasting side characters that still feel like they belong in your world.

At the end of the day, a great supporting cast feels like people who have lives beyond the scenes they're in. The audience should believe they have routines, regrets, dreams, and pasts—even if we only get glimpses. They don't just complete your protagonist. They complete your story. And when you build them with intention, detail, and emotional dimension—whether you do that alone or with the help of ChatGPT—you're creating a series that feels like a living, breathing world. One that viewers won't want to leave.

Defining the Tone and Mood of Your Series

Tone and mood are like the invisible glue holding your series together. They guide the audience's emotional experience and help set expectations from the very first frame. If plot is what happens, and character is who it happens to, then tone is *how* it feels while it's happening. It's the difference between a high-stakes drama and a dark comedy, even if they share the same plot. It's the reason why two shows about detectives can feel completely different—one gritty and oppressive, the other sharp and absurd. When you define the tone and mood of your series early, you're not just making a stylistic decision—you're building trust with your audience. They want to know what kind of ride they're in for. And once you've established that, you get to keep delivering or play against it in ways that feel intentional.

So what exactly *is* tone, and how is it different from mood? Think of tone as the voice of your show—it's the overall attitude or emotional lens through which the story is told. Is it cynical? Hopeful? Sarcastic? Brutal? Gentle? Mood, on the other hand, is what the audience feels as a result. A show with a warm tone might evoke a comforting mood. A satirical tone might create a biting or awkward mood. Both are crucial in creating a consistent viewing experience, and both are shaped by your writing, directing, pacing, music, color palette, and even casting choices.

When you're working with ChatGPT to shape your pilot, one of the smartest moves you can make early in the process is to define the tone and mood in words. Try asking, "What would the tone of this series be if it's a deadpan satire versus an emotional character drama?" You'll get breakdowns that help you see how everything from dialogue to scene transitions would need to shift depending on the tone you choose. You can even take a scene you've already written and ask ChatGPT to rewrite it in a different tone. The contrast will teach you a lot about what tone *feels* like in action.

Let's say your story is about a woman who returns to her hometown to uncover the truth behind her brother's death. This could go in so many tonal directions. You could go for moody and melancholic, leaning into long silences, subtle expressions, and haunting visuals. Or you could play it as a dark comedy, full of awkward reunions, repressed secrets, and inappropriate laughter. Or maybe it's a gritty mystery with a hardboiled edge and bursts of violence. The plot doesn't change, but the experience of watching it does. And tone is the reason why.

Once you pick a tone, everything else has to line up. Dialogue, especially, is one of the clearest indicators of tone. A sharp, witty script tells the viewer to expect humor or satire. Sparse, clipped exchanges set a more serious tone. ChatGPT is great for tuning your dialogue. You can say, "Rewrite this scene in a dry, sardonic tone," or "Make this conversation more emotionally charged without becoming melodramatic," and it will give you options that reflect those tonal choices. That's how you refine the feel of your show, one line at a time.

Your scene descriptions also help set the tone. A serious drama might use language that's elegant, restrained, even poetic. A gritty urban crime show might use sharper, grittier language. A whimsical fantasy might lean into playful or surreal imagery. Don't underestimate how your writing style influences tone. You can test this by asking ChatGPT to generate descriptions for a location or action in different tones. For example, "Describe a character walking into a bar in a noir tone versus a romantic comedy tone." Seeing the difference in phrasing will sharpen your instincts about what kind of world you're building.

Another major part of tone is pacing. A slow-burn psychological thriller lives in drawn-out silences and lingering shots. A snappy workplace comedy moves fast and doesn't dwell. If your tone is inconsistent with your pacing, the show can feel disjointed. If you're not sure how to balance this, ChatGPT can help by analyzing your scene rhythm. You can ask,

"Does this scene feel too slow for a suspenseful tone?" or "How can I make this moment land with more energy while keeping the tone consistent?" The AI will help you shape the emotional tempo.

Tone also bleeds into character. In a show with a satirical tone, characters might be exaggerated versions of real people—flawed, ridiculous, heightened. In a grounded drama, they'll be complex, nuanced, and understated. Your cast needs to match the emotional rules of your show. If you drop a cartoonish character into a gritty crime story, it'll break the tone—unless that clash is intentional. You can work with ChatGPT to match character voices to tone by asking, "Does this character feel too broad for the show's tone?" or "Give me dialogue examples that better fit a melancholic tone."

Music and visual design aren't part of the script per se, but they still inform tone, especially if you're developing the pilot with a clear vision. If there's a specific vibe—lo-fi, synth-heavy, orchestral, minimalist—you can describe that mood in your scene headers or write your script with a musical rhythm in mind. Ask ChatGPT for a playlist that matches your show's tone, or visual references to help articulate the atmosphere. These tools help build a cohesive creative identity for your series.

And don't forget about the *emotional honesty* of your tone. If you're writing comedy, are the characters still emotionally real, or are they jokes with legs? If it's drama, is the intensity earned, or is it over the top? Whatever tone you choose, make sure it supports your theme and lets the characters live and breathe. Use ChatGPT to spot tonal missteps. Say, "Does this scene feel emotionally honest for a dark comedy?" or "How can I ground this character in a heightened tonal world?" That kind of question leads to better execution.

Tone is also where your series stands out. It's what makes *Stranger Things* feel nostalgic but scary, *Barry* feel hilarious and tragic, *Succession* feel icy and absurd. You're not just telling a story—you're creating a *feeling*. And that feeling is what brings audiences back.

So define it. Name it. Play with it. Push it. And once you find it, lean all the way in. Because when tone and mood are dialled in, your show doesn't just make sense—it *sings*. And ChatGPT is here to help you stay in tune every step of the way.

Using ChatGPT to Explore Character Backstories

Backstory is the invisible thread that pulls your characters through every moment of your story. It's the thing they carry with them into every conversation, every decision, every mistake. You might not show all of it on the page, especially in a pilot, but it informs everything—how they speak, what they want, what they fear, and what they're hiding. When backstory is done well, it makes your characters feel lived-in, like they existed long before the pilot started and will continue after the credits roll. And the process of discovering and shaping those hidden histories becomes a lot easier—and a lot more fun—when you're using ChatGPT.

Most writers think of backstory as something that has to be written in isolation—a long document you do before the actual writing begins. But what makes ChatGPT so powerful is that you don't have to treat it like homework. You can build your character's past dynamically and conversationally. You can toss out ideas, test different paths, and refine the emotional details in real time, without getting bogged down in overthinking. It's like having a writing partner who never runs out of patience or creative fuel.

Let's say you've got a basic character idea: a paramedic in a major city who secretly wants to quit and become a painter. That's the tip of the iceberg. But why? Why art? Why now? What's the story underneath that tension? Open ChatGPT and start a dialogue. Say, "Help me explore the backstory of a paramedic named Evan who's afraid to leave his job even though he dreams of becoming an artist." Immediately, you'll start getting questions and ideas in return—maybe Evan's father was a firefighter who died in the line of duty, and Evan feels like he owes something to that legacy. Maybe he failed out of art school when he was younger and thinks he's missed his chance. Or maybe he once saved a child who drew him a picture, and that moment quietly changed everything.

Each of these ideas opens doors. You don't have to pick just one—you can explore all of them. You can ask for variations: "Give me five reasons Evan might feel trapped in his job," or "What traumatic event in his past could explain his fear of change?" ChatGPT can provide you with dramatic events, quiet emotional moments, or even subtle patterns in his life that help shape who he is now. You don't need to use every detail, but the more you understand, the more confidently you can write his choices and reactions.

Backstory also helps define relationships. Say your lead character has a complicated dynamic with a sibling. You don't want to explain that in exposition—you want to show it in behavior. So start by asking ChatGPT, "What's a backstory between two siblings who love each other but don't speak anymore?" You'll get a variety of emotionally loaded events—betrayals, family secrets, diverging values—that can manifest subtly in your pilot. One sibling might constantly interrupt. The other might refuse to make eye contact. Those little moments land harder when they're built on a foundation the audience can *feel*, even if they don't fully understand it yet.

Backstory isn't just about what happened. It's about how that history still *lives* in the character. A character who was abandoned might now sabotage every relationship. A character who lost a sibling might become overly protective. A character who once lived through war might always know where the exits are in a room. These are emotional behaviors, not exposition. ChatGPT can help you brainstorm behaviors and traits that reflect internal scars. You can say, "What are some subtle ways a person with abandonment trauma might behave in everyday life?" and you'll get real, textured material that grounds your characters in truth.

You can also ask ChatGPT to help you create character timelines. Ask for a year-by-year breakdown of your character's life. Not because you'll include every detail in your pilot, but because *you* need to know what they've been through. Say,

"Give me a life timeline for a 35-year-old woman who grew up in foster care, served in the military, and is now a private investigator," and watch as a whole life unfolds. Then you can highlight the key beats that shaped her worldview—and find clever, understated ways to reflect those events in her present.

Let's not forget the power of secrets. A great character almost always has something they're hiding—from the world, from someone close to them, or from themselves. You can use ChatGPT to brainstorm secrets that are emotionally or dramatically explosive. Say, "What's a secret that would quietly eat away at a character's confidence?" or "What's a truth this character is refusing to admit about their past?" The answers might inspire entire episodes or shape the season's emotional arc.

And here's where things get even more useful: ChatGPT can help you *weave* backstory into your pilot without slowing down the pacing. You can paste a scene and ask, "How can I reveal this character's backstory through action instead of dialogue?" or "What's a visual way to hint at this past trauma?" Instead of info dumps, you get story beats—quiet gestures, charged silences, or lines of dialogue that land like veiled confessions. That's how you keep things moving without sacrificing depth.

You can also run parallel backstories to explore character relationships. Let's say you're writing two characters who are partners in a high-stakes job—say, spies, doctors, or bounty hunters. You can ask ChatGPT to create a backstory for each that intersects in a dramatic or ironic way. Maybe one saved the other's life years ago, but neither of them has talked about it since. Maybe they betrayed each other once but never acknowledged it. These shared or overlapping histories give your scenes weight and texture, and they're often where the show's emotional punch really lives.

And remember—backstory doesn't need to be fixed forever. Just like in real life, the way a character sees their past can evolve. Maybe they believe their parent abandoned them, but later discover it was more complicated. Maybe they think they caused someone harm, but they were misinformed. ChatGPT can help you explore those narrative reversals and the emotional fallout that comes with them.

At the end of the day, using ChatGPT to explore character backstories is like having an endless character workshop at your fingertips. You're not staring at a blank page, trying to pull trauma out of thin air. You're shaping lives with intention. You're digging beneath the surface, one layer at a time, until your characters don't just feel believable—they feel *real*. And when they show up in your pilot, even for a few lines, the audience will sense that depth. They'll lean in. They'll want to know more. And that's when your characters stop being words on a page—and start living in someone else's imagination.

The Power of Dialogue in the Pilot Script

Dialogue is one of the most powerful tools you have in a pilot script. It's the voice of your characters, the vehicle for story, the hidden doorway to theme, and the thing that brings everything to life on screen. It's how we get to know who your characters really are, not by what they say, but by *how* they say it—what they reveal, what they hide, and how they interact with the world and each other. A single line of dialogue can introduce a character, shift a relationship, set the tone of the show, and launch a conflict, all in under five seconds. That's the kind of efficient storytelling that a great pilot needs. And with ChatGPT, you've got an on-demand creative partner who can help you sharpen, test, and elevate every word that comes out of your characters' mouths.

Dialogue in a pilot has a special role because it's doing double-duty. It has to sound natural while also carrying a lot of weight. You're not just having characters chit-chat. You're establishing dynamics, tone, exposition, humor, tension, world rules, and personality. In a typical scene, dialogue might take a back seat to visuals or action, but in a pilot, especially in television, it's often the main event. People are tuning in to *meet* your characters—how they talk is often their first impression.

The key to writing strong dialogue in your pilot is to make it do something. Every line needs to serve a purpose. It should reveal something—about the speaker, about the other character, about the world, or about what's coming. And it should do that without sounding like it's trying too hard. That balance between natural and meaningful is tricky, but that's where ChatGPT can help. You can take a scene and ask, "How can this dialogue better reflect the character's fear of abandonment?" or "Rewrite this exchange to show rising tension without stating it directly." ChatGPT will give you fresh takes that keep the subtext alive while trimming away the fluff.

One of the most useful ways to use ChatGPT when working on dialogue is to find each character's voice. Not everyone should sound the same. Your lead might be sarcastic and guarded, while their best friend is earnest and talks too fast. One character might never finish a sentence. Another might never say what they actually mean. You can ask ChatGPT to help craft distinct voices by feeding in a character's personality and background and saying, "What does someone like this sound like in conversation?" or "Write a sample monologue in this character's voice." That kind of modeling is a great way to find your rhythm.

Think about *how* people speak in real life. They interrupt, they dodge, they joke when they're nervous, they lie without blinking, they circle around what they actually want to say. Great dialogue reflects this messiness while still pushing the story forward. In a pilot, you want to capture the feeling that these characters existed long before page one—and will continue existing long after the scene ends. You don't want to write lines that simply serve the plot. You want dialogue that reveals character through conflict, behavior, and voice. Ask ChatGPT to generate five ways a character might avoid answering a direct question without being obvious, and you'll find more organic ways to layer emotion into the scene.

Another mistake to avoid in your pilot is using dialogue as a delivery system for exposition. New writers often load up conversations with world-building details that nobody would say out loud. If your character says, "As you know, since our father disappeared in 1994 after the fire," it sounds clunky because real people don't talk like that. Instead, use *implied* exposition—let the audience fill in the gaps. You can use ChatGPT to rework expository dialogue into something more natural by asking, "Rewrite this line to imply backstory without stating it directly," or "How can this character hint at their resentment without saying it outright?" The answers will often point you to more subtle, emotionally honest ways to convey the same information.

Subtext is where dialogue becomes powerful. When characters are saying one thing and meaning another, the scene becomes more layered, more alive. Conflict simmers. Relationships get complicated. Audiences love reading between the lines. So build scenes where your characters are holding something back. Use ChatGPT to experiment with levels of subtext. Ask it to write the same scene three ways: one with surface-level honesty, one with passive-aggressive tension, and one with loaded silence. You'll start to see how meaning shifts with tone and intent—even if the words stay almost the same.

Don't forget rhythm. Dialogue has music to it. It can be fast, jagged, looping, or painfully still. The way characters speak creates momentum, and in a pilot, that momentum is everything. Snappy dialogue can make a drama crackle. Lingering pauses can make a comedy feel profound. Varying the pace between characters can make scenes more dynamic. You can even test this with ChatGPT by saying, "Make this scene tighter and more rhythmically sharp," or "Add pauses and beats to slow this exchange down emotionally." You'll see how pacing affects tone and tension.

Humor is another major tool in your dialogue arsenal. Even serious shows benefit from moments of levity. Humor makes characters relatable and moments memorable. And it doesn't have to be punchlines—it can be awkward timing, blunt honesty, or poetic irony. Use ChatGPT to test different types of humor. Ask, "Rewrite this exchange with dry wit," or "Add a moment of absurdity between two serious characters." You might land on a character's signature voice just by playing with tone.

Finally, remember that great dialogue leaves room for silence. Some of the best lines in television history aren't lines at all—they're the things characters *don't* say. The glance across the table. The interrupted confession. The pause before the lie. When used right, silence is louder than any monologue. You can even ask ChatGPT, "What's a moment in this scene that might be more powerful without words?" and build tension through restraint.

At the end of the day, dialogue in your pilot is about control. It's about knowing what your characters want and using every word—or silence—to get them closer or further away from that goal. It's about conflict, emotion, rhythm, and reveal. And when you use ChatGPT to test, tweak, and explore your lines, you don't waste time guessing. You're working with precision. You're shaping moments that stick.

So when you sit down to write those early scenes, don't just think about what the characters need to say. Think about what the *audience* needs to feel. Because when dialogue is crafted with care, your characters don't just talk—they come alive. And once they do, your show truly begins.

Plotting the Pilot: One Scene at a Time

Writing a pilot can feel overwhelming when you're staring down the entire thing as one massive project. You're trying to introduce the world, the protagonist, the supporting characters, the main conflict, the tone, the genre—and do all of that while keeping the story moving, the pacing tight, and the dialogue sharp. It's enough to melt anyone's brain. But here's the truth: you don't have to write the whole pilot at once. You just have to write one scene. Then the next. Then the next. When you approach plotting scene by scene, the pressure drops, your focus sharpens, and suddenly, you're building something solid, one step at a time. And when you've got ChatGPT to help you walk through each of those scenes, you've got a writing partner who's there to test ideas, fill in gaps, and keep the momentum going.

A TV pilot is usually about 50 to 60 pages for an hour-long drama and 22 to 35 pages for a half-hour comedy. No matter the length, every scene needs to earn its place. Every scene needs to move the story forward, reveal something important, or shift the dynamics between characters. If it's not doing one of those things, it's dead weight. That's why plotting scene by scene is such an effective method. It forces you to ask, "Why is this moment here?" If you can't answer that, you either need to change it—or cut it.

The best place to start is with your protagonist. What's their emotional state in scene one? And what do you want their state to be in the final scene of the pilot? That's your beginning and end. Once you know that arc, you can begin plotting the path between them. Start by asking ChatGPT to help: "Create a ten-scene outline for a pilot where the main character begins confident and ends completely uncertain." That simple prompt can help shape the emotional skeleton of your episode. From there, you fill in the muscles—what actually happens, who's involved, and what's at stake.

Once you've got your basic scene roadmap, start developing each scene on its own terms. Don't worry about transitions or the bigger picture just yet. Ask yourself, "What is the purpose of this scene?" and "What changes by the end of it?" Maybe a relationship shifts, a piece of information is revealed, or a new problem shows up. Ask ChatGPT to help clarify or enhance that scene's function. You can say, "This is a scene where the protagonist meets the antagonist. What's a subtle way to build tension without making it obvious they're enemies yet?" You'll get suggestions for beats, gestures, or lines of dialogue that give the scene depth and direction.

Let's say you're working on scene three, where your protagonist lies to their boss about something major. You know the lie will come back to haunt them in episode five, but how do you make this scene matter now? Ask ChatGPT, "How can I make this lie feel loaded, even though the consequences don't show up until later?" It might suggest a look from a side character who overhears. A suspicious pause from the boss. A flash of guilt that interrupts the flow. Now that scene has tension—not just in the moment, but layered with future stakes.

Another benefit of scene-by-scene plotting is that it helps manage tone. One scene might be tense, the next comedic, the next quiet and reflective. You don't want all your scenes to feel the same, but you also don't want wild tonal whiplash. Use ChatGPT to help balance that out. Ask, "What's a light scene I could place after a heavy emotional beat?" or "How can I carry tension from one scene into the next without repeating the same emotional note?" These small pacing adjustments make your pilot feel intentional and alive.

Also, think of each scene as its own tiny story. It should have a beginning, middle, and end—even if it's only a couple of minutes long. Someone wants something. There's resistance or discovery. Then the scene ends in a different place than it started. That shift is what keeps the audience engaged. You can use ChatGPT to sharpen this by saying, "What's a mini-conflict that could play out between these two characters in this scene?" or "How can this moment end in a surprising but inevitable way?" That last part—*surprising but inevitable*—is the sweet spot of great storytelling.

Dialogue in each scene should be driven by intent. Every character wants something in that moment, even if they don't say it out loud. They're trying to get information, gain power, protect themselves, or connect. That intent gives the scene its spine. Ask ChatGPT to help uncover what each character wants in the scene. Say, "What does this character want in this scene—and what are they afraid the other character will discover?" That instantly adds tension and purpose to even the quietest moments.

Visual rhythm matters too. Not every scene should be talking heads in a room. Some should move. Some should shift location. Some should play with silence or background action. ChatGPT can help you reimagine static scenes with prompts like, "What's a more dynamic setting for this conversation?" or "How can I use the environment to mirror the characters' emotional state in this scene?" Those little shifts make your pilot feel more cinematic and fluid.

And as you build scene by scene, keep a living outline. After writing each scene, step back and update your scene list. What's changed? What still needs to happen? Are you building to something? You can ask ChatGPT to track your structure: "Based on these scenes, what's the act break?" or "What could be a strong midpoint twist to shift the energy?" It's like having a writer's room inside your laptop—always ready to bounce ideas, adjust structure, and help you keep the big picture clear while you focus on the scene in front of you.

The beauty of plotting your pilot one scene at a time is that it gives you freedom and focus. You're not trying to write everything perfectly at once. You're building something piece by piece, like a sculptor shaping clay. You're free to explore, make mistakes, throw scenes out, and write them again better. With ChatGPT there to help you explore variations, keep things moving, and challenge your first instincts, you'll find that plotting becomes less of a puzzle and more of a game.

So take a breath, stop worrying about the entire script, and ask yourself—what's the next scene? Who's in it? What's changing? Why does it matter? Write that. Then write the one after. And before you know it, your pilot will be more than a plan—it'll be a story. A living, breathing story told one moment, one scene, one decision at a time.

Pacing: How to Keep the Energy Up

Pacing is one of those things that doesn't get talked about enough when writing a TV pilot, but it's often the difference between someone watching the whole episode or bailing after ten minutes. Good pacing isn't about speed—it's about rhythm. It's how the story moves, how the emotional beats rise and fall, how tension builds and releases, and how your viewer feels like something's always happening, even in the quiet moments. A well-paced pilot is like a song you can't stop listening to—it keeps pulling you forward. And the best part is, you don't have to rely on instinct alone. With ChatGPT, you can test your pacing scene by scene and beat by beat, making sure your pilot flows with the kind of momentum that hooks viewers from start to finish.

First, let's define what pacing actually is in a screenplay. It's not just how long scenes are, though that's part of it. It's how long we stay in one emotional state, how quickly problems escalate, how often we shift perspectives or settings, how tightly dialogue is written, and how much tension is created or relieved. Pacing is also about expectation. If the viewer feels like they're waiting too long for something to happen—or too much is happening with no emotional weight—they'll check out. So pacing is really about balance.

A common mistake in early drafts is either cramming in too much information upfront or dragging through setup with no sense of urgency. That's why starting your pilot with some kind of hook—a question, a twist, a moment of tension—is essential. It doesn't need to be huge, but it needs to suggest that something bigger is coming. You want the audience thinking, "I need to know what happens next." You can use ChatGPT to help generate multiple versions of your opening scene, each with a different tone or structure, and compare how each one sets the pacing. Ask, "What's a stronger opening beat to make this story feel more urgent?" or "Give me a version of this cold open that feels more high-stakes."

One simple way to manage pacing is to think in terms of tension and release. You can't keep everything high-intensity the whole time or the audience gets numb. And if you stay in calm, quiet scenes for too long, they start to feel static. Alternating between tension-building scenes and more reflective or comedic moments creates a flow. Think of it like waves—each rise in tension builds toward a larger swell, and each break gives the audience space to absorb what just happened. You can ask ChatGPT to help structure this: "Where should the emotional high points and quiet moments fall in this pilot to maintain strong pacing?"

Another tool is changing up the type of scenes you're writing. Don't follow a dramatic scene with another dramatic scene on the same beat unless that's the whole point. Mix dialogue-heavy scenes with action, movement, or mystery. Change settings. Change who's in the scene. Shift the focus of the conflict. Ask ChatGPT, "What's a good way to shift energy after this emotional argument scene?" and it might give you a small win, a twist, or even a moment of dark humor to break the intensity without killing the momentum.

Dialogue is a major player in pacing. If your characters ramble or the conversation doesn't shift or escalate, the scene starts to feel long—even if it's only a page or two. Tight dialogue keeps things sharp. Characters should enter a scene wanting something, and the back-and-forth should either move them closer to or further from that goal. Use ChatGPT to cut the fat from dialogue by asking, "How can I make this exchange ten percent tighter without losing meaning?" or "What's a sharper way to raise the stakes in this conversation?" That kind of revision can turn a decent scene into a page-turner.

Scene length is worth watching too, but not in a rigid "every scene must be two pages" kind of way. Some scenes can live in silence and stretch out, but they need to *earn* that space with atmosphere or emotional weight. If a scene feels like it's dragging, ask ChatGPT, "What is this scene doing for the plot or character arc, and how could it do it more efficiently?" Often, trimming half a page or starting the scene later in the action can make a huge difference.

Another pacing trick is layering multiple threads at once. Instead of focusing all your energy on just one storyline, you can cut between an A plot, B plot, and sometimes even a C plot. These threads should connect thematically or emotionally, even if they seem unrelated at first. By jumping between them, you keep the pace moving and build suspense across different parts of your story world. ChatGPT can help you structure this: "How do I interweave three plotlines across a single pilot episode without losing clarity?" It'll help you balance time, tension, and payoff across each arc.

Pacing is also about surprises. The audience should never feel like they know exactly what's going to happen next. You want to subvert their expectations just enough to keep them engaged. If your pilot is feeling too predictable, you can ask ChatGPT to help shake things up: "What's an unexpected complication that could shift the direction of this scene without changing the overall plot?" These little disruptions keep the viewer leaning in instead of leaning back.

And let's not forget the last few pages of your pilot. You want to end with something that feels like a jolt—an emotional or narrative charge that makes people need to see episode two. This doesn't mean you always need a cliffhanger. It just means the last beat should feel like the opening of a new door, not the closing of one. Ask ChatGPT to pitch endings that feel like setups. Say, "What's a final scene that shifts the story or character arc in a surprising but meaningful way?" You'll get ideas that elevate the ending from a quiet fade-out to a power move.

The beauty of using ChatGPT while managing pacing is that you're never stuck in slow motion. You can test your script's rhythm in real time. You can ask it to flag scenes that drag, help inject more urgency, or even restructure the order of scenes for better flow. You don't need to guess if your pacing is working—you can actively tune it like an instrument.

So if your pilot ever starts to feel like it's dragging, don't panic. Zoom in. Focus on one scene. One beat. One transition. Ask, "What needs to shift here?" Then adjust. Rebalance. Keep the energy up—not just with action or speed, but with emotional charge, dynamic change, and a sense that something is always happening. When you master that rhythm, your audience will ride every wave—and they won't want to stop.

Visualizing Scenes While Writing with ChatGPT

Writing a pilot script is a deeply visual experience—even if it's done on a blank page with only black text. You're not just telling a story, you're designing a *television show*, which means you need to *see* it while you write it. Not in a vague, mental-image kind of way, but in detailed, frame-by-frame clarity. What's the camera seeing? What's in the room? What's the weather like? Where's the character standing? What does their face do before they say a word? These are the details that make scenes feel alive, cinematic, and emotionally rich. And the great news is that ChatGPT is uniquely good at helping you visualize these moments as you write, because it thinks in possibilities—and it can describe them as vividly as you ask it to.

When you write, you're not just creating dialogue and action—you're directing on the page. But unlike directing on set, you're doing it with pure imagination. If you're stuck trying to picture how a scene should look, feel, or unfold, ChatGPT can act as your concept artist, your set designer, even your cinematographer. You don't need to go in with a fully formed idea. You can just say, "Describe a tense dinner scene between two estranged siblings," and instantly get a vivid layout of a dimly lit room, mismatched silverware, a flickering candle, awkward glances, clinking forks, and a thousand unsaid words. All of that becomes the backdrop for your dialogue—and the vibe for the scene.

The key to visual storytelling is writing in a way that lets the reader *see* what's happening, without overloading the script with prose. You want to be economical but evocative. ChatGPT can help you find the balance. Try feeding in a block of action and asking, "Can you rewrite this scene with more visual detail but keep it under five lines?" It'll give you suggestions that enhance the atmosphere without bloating the script. It's not about writing a novel—it's about writing a visual moment that jumps off the page.

Let's say your character is walking into a police station. You could write, "INT. POLICE STATION – DAY," and leave it at that. Or you could go further: "The walls are pale green and buzzing with fluorescent light. A busted vending machine hums in the corner. A teenager sits handcuffed to a chair, staring at the floor. A desk fan rattles like it's about to fall apart." Now we feel the world. We're *in* the scene. You can ask ChatGPT, "What are some small visual details that could make this police station feel specific and slightly surreal?" and you'll get ideas you hadn't considered—stuff that sparks tone and character just by being there.

The same goes for physical action. Visualizing how characters move through a scene adds dynamism. Don't just write that they "argue in the kitchen"—write how one paces, how the other cuts vegetables with too much force, how the tension lives in body language. Ask ChatGPT to add non-verbal beats to a conversation. Say, "What are some subtle actions a character might do while lying to someone?" Suddenly, your dialogue gets layered with behavior—and your scene becomes more watchable, more cinematic, and more real.

Camera direction is usually avoided in standard spec scripts unless it's integral to the storytelling, but that doesn't mean you can't write *cinematically*. Think about what the audience sees. What's revealed in the frame? What's withheld? What's the opening shot that sets the emotional tone? You can describe it in a sentence without ever saying "we see." Something like: "Her fingers tremble as she lines up prescription bottles on the sink—each one perfectly spaced, except for the empty one." You've just written a shot that says *a lot* visually without being technical.

You can even use ChatGPT to explore variations of the same scene. Say, "Give me three different visual ways to show someone feeling alone in a crowded space." You might get a version set in a subway station, a party, and a grocery store—all different, all visually loaded. You pick the one that hits hardest. That's how you write with style and intention instead of just coverage.

And don't forget that emotional tone is visual too. A breakup in the pouring rain feels different than one in a sterile, fluorescent-lit waiting room. The same line of dialogue can land wildly differently depending on what the character sees—or doesn't see—at that moment. Ask ChatGPT, "What setting would intensify this emotional beat without using cliché?" or "What's a symbolic visual element I could place in this scene to suggest betrayal?" These details elevate the writing from functional to *artful*.

Another tip: use visuals to express theme. If your show is about surveillance and secrets, let the world reflect that. Glimpses of people behind blinds, reflections in mirrors, eyes in paintings—these aren't just props. They reinforce your ideas without a word being said. Ask ChatGPT to brainstorm visual metaphors tied to your theme, and you'll get a ton of layered possibilities that make your scenes do double duty.

Sometimes, especially when writing for genre—sci-fi, horror, fantasy—writers get overwhelmed by the need to build big worlds. But world-building starts with detail, not exposition. You don't have to explain how the tech works. Just show a character casually using it. You don't need a history lesson about the war. Just show its effects in the landscape or the way people move around each other. Ask ChatGPT, "How can I show this world's rules visually without any exposition?" and you'll get clean, efficient, powerful ideas that bring the world to life *through the frame*, not through dialogue.

One more trick: treat your transitions like mini-movies. Instead of cutting from one scene to the next with no connective tissue, ask yourself how one moment *leads* to the next emotionally and visually. A character walking into fog. A dropped object that cuts to a similar shape in the next scene. These little choices add texture and help pacing too. Ask ChatGPT to suggest visual transitions based on tone, and you'll get ideas that keep your pilot flowing like a show, not a series of disconnected events.

At the end of the day, writing with visual intent is what separates a script from a story. It's the difference between someone reading your pilot and thinking, "This is interesting," and someone thinking, "I can *see* this show." With ChatGPT, you're not just imagining alone—you're collaborating with a tool that can throw visual references, describe cinematic moments, and help you see the scene before you even write it. So next time you get stuck, don't just ask, "What happens next?" Ask, "What *does it look like* when it happens?" And let ChatGPT help you build something the audience won't just understand—they'll *feel*. Scene by scene. Frame by frame. Until the world you're writing is no longer just on the page—but alive in the mind's eye.

Weaving in Subplots without Losing Focus

Subplots are the secret spice that make your pilot feel like the start of something rich, layered, and worth returning to. They add depth to your world, dimension to your characters, and the kind of texture that transforms a single story into a series. But they're also tricky. Add too many subplots too soon, and your pilot feels bloated or chaotic. Lean too hard on one, and it can start to feel like a distraction from the main plot. The trick is to introduce subplots with purpose, timing, and subtlety—making sure they serve the core story rather than splintering away from it. And with ChatGPT, you've got a tool that helps you keep that delicate balance in check while still allowing your creativity to run wild.

The first rule of weaving in subplots is this: the subplot must reflect, contrast with, or complicate the main plot. It should be connected emotionally, thematically, or structurally. If it's just running alongside the story without interacting with it, it'll feel like filler. But if the subplot shows another side of the protagonist's life, or provides insight into a theme, or creates emotional stakes for a future payoff, it suddenly becomes essential. You can use ChatGPT to vet your subplot ideas by asking, "How does this subplot reinforce the main story or theme?" or "What's a smart way for this subplot to collide with the main plot by episode three?" That kind of analysis keeps you from going off-track.

Subplots are a great way to explore supporting characters and broaden your world without losing sight of your protagonist. Maybe your lead is trying to land a high-profile job, while their younger sibling is struggling to keep their corner store afloat. The two plots don't seem connected—until your lead's job turns out to be with the company trying to buy the block and bulldoze the store. Now the subplot is no longer separate—it's *pressure*. It forces choices, deepens conflict, and makes the stakes feel more personal. ChatGPT can help generate these intersections by asking, "How could these two storylines affect each other in an organic way?"

Timing is everything. You don't need to cram every subplot into the first ten minutes. Let your main story establish its footing first. Introduce subplots naturally through character behavior and interaction. For example, a flirtation at work might hint at a romantic subplot. A voicemail from a parent might suggest a family issue. These little seeds don't need full scenes right away—they just need to be planted. You can use ChatGPT to help stagger the introduction of subplots. Ask, "In what scene would it feel natural to introduce this subplot without pulling focus?" or "What's a way to hint at this character's hidden agenda before revealing it fully later?" That way, the subplot simmers instead of stealing attention.

Subplots also thrive on character motivation. If your character's actions in the subplot reveal something new about them—or push them toward (or away from) a major decision—they're doing the right work. Maybe your protagonist is keeping a secret relationship on the side. That subplot might not be about the main conflict, but it shows us how they handle truth, loyalty, and risk. Now when they're faced with a big moral choice in the main plot, we already know how they're wired. You can ask ChatGPT, "What's a subplot that would reveal my protagonist's fear of vulnerability?" or "How can this subplot create internal tension for the main character later in the pilot?"

Another smart use of subplots is to expand your world. A subplot can show the social, political, or cultural context that your main character lives in without them having to explain it. In *The Wire*, for example, the various subplots don't just make the world feel bigger—they show how systems of power, law, and survival overlap in every corner. You can use ChatGPT to help world-build through subplot. Ask, "What subplot could show the economic pressure of this community without being preachy?" or "How can a subplot reveal the larger system my character is trapped in?" Now you're enriching the world while keeping it grounded in character.

Keep in mind that the tone of your subplot should match or intentionally contrast with the tone of your main story. A subplot that's too goofy in an otherwise grounded thriller can pull the audience out of the story—unless the contrast is used to highlight the absurdity of the world or to give the audience a necessary emotional release. If you're unsure, you can ask ChatGPT, "Does this subplot feel tonally consistent with the rest of the script?" or "What's a way to bring levity to this subplot without breaking the mood of the main plot?" It'll help you calibrate your tone so that everything feels part of the same universe.

One underrated trick to managing subplots is to make sure they also *end* or shift at the right moment. Subplots shouldn't just fizzle out. They need beats—twists, escalations, revelations. You don't need to resolve them in the pilot, but you should signal that they're going somewhere. Use ChatGPT to structure your subplot arcs: "What's a three-beat structure for this subplot that aligns with the main plot's tension curve?" That way, you're building to moments that feel earned, rather than randomly inserted.

And of course, subplots can and should collide. Let two characters with totally different subplots crash into each other unexpectedly. Let someone's personal issue become the key to solving a problem in the main story. These kinds of overlaps are satisfying because they make the world feel interconnected and dynamic. Ask ChatGPT, "What's a surprising way these two subplots could overlap by the end of the pilot?" or "How could a background character's subplot become crucial to the protagonist's success or failure?"

The goal isn't to pack your pilot with endless threads. It's to give the audience the sense that this is a world full of moving parts. That there are stories waiting to unfold beyond the frame. That the characters are living lives that don't pause when the camera cuts away. ChatGPT helps you track all those layers while keeping your focus sharp. You can build, test, and refine every subplot before it ever hits the page, which means your pilot will feel tight, alive, and full of momentum.

So don't fear subplots—just be strategic. Make them work in tandem with your core story. Let them echo, reflect, challenge, and deepen the main plot. With the right balance, your pilot becomes more than just a beginning—it becomes a world people want to return to again and again. And that's how great series are born.

Laying the Foundation for the Series Arc

Writing a pilot episode is not just about telling a great one-off story—it's about planting seeds that can grow into a full season, or better yet, an entire series. While the plot of the pilot needs to be engaging on its own, it also has to quietly (or not-so-quietly) lay the foundation for what's coming next. You're not just introducing characters—you're introducing potential. The pilot needs to promise something bigger, more complex, and worth watching week after week. And that's where the series arc comes in. Whether you're working in drama, comedy, sci-fi, or even anthology, thinking ahead—even just loosely—about where the story *could* go gives your pilot direction and depth. And with ChatGPT in your corner, you can map out the future while staying grounded in the now.

The series arc is the emotional and narrative journey that stretches beyond episode one. It's the long game. It's the big problem that won't be solved anytime soon. It's the inner transformation of your protagonist and the larger shift in the world they live in. In most great shows, the series arc is about something *changing*—in society, in a system, in a relationship, or in a person. That change is slow, sometimes painful, sometimes thrilling. And it starts with small moments in the pilot.

So how do you begin to lay this groundwork without turning your pilot into a five-season outline? You focus on *implications*. What questions are you raising? What mystery are you hinting at? What contradiction are you exposing? Your audience doesn't need the answers right away—they just need to feel like there *are* answers to be found. That sense of depth keeps them hooked. You can ask ChatGPT, "What larger mystery could be hinted at in the background of this pilot?" or "How can this character's small decision ripple across an entire season?" These kinds of prompts help you write with long-term resonance.

Think of your pilot like the first chapter of a novel. It needs to introduce the story world, establish the rules (and where they might break), and set up the first turning point. But it should also contain a few subtle (or not-so-subtle) cracks in the foundation—clues that all is not as it seems. Maybe your hero wins in the pilot, but it costs them something they don't realize yet. Maybe a background character has more power than it first appears. Maybe a piece of throwaway dialogue hints at a buried secret. These are all breadcrumbs leading to the bigger picture.

One of the best ways to explore your series arc is by looking at your protagonist's emotional journey. Where are they at the start of the pilot—and where do you *want* them to be by the end of the season or series? That contrast gives you your arc. If they begin as naive, maybe they end as cynical. If they start emotionally closed off, maybe they end in a state of unexpected connection. Now the question becomes: how do you hint at that evolution in episode one without rushing it? Ask ChatGPT, "What early behavior could subtly foreshadow this character's future transformation?" and you'll get concrete ways to layer in the foundation.

The series arc isn't just about your main character, though. It's also about the story engine. What system or situation is your show examining? Maybe it's a flawed justice system, a collapsing marriage, a haunted town, or a corrupt corporation. Your pilot should set the rules of that world—but it should also show the *tension* within those rules. That tension is what drives future episodes. ChatGPT can help you dig into the system at play by asking, "What system is this show exposing or challenging?" or "What recurring obstacle could power multiple storylines across a season?"

You also want to build flexibility into your arc. You don't need to know every beat of every episode, but you should have a sense of the shape. Where are your characters likely to clash? What truth is waiting to be uncovered? What event could blow up the whole premise by midseason? You can ask ChatGPT to outline possible long-term arcs: "What's a five-episode escalation of this central conflict?" or "What could be a midseason twist that redefines the main character's journey?" These outlines aren't blueprints—you can change them—but they give you structure to build from.

One subtle but powerful way to lay a foundation is through unanswered questions. Who is that mysterious person watching the protagonist? Why is the old file missing from the archive? What did that one character almost say before cutting themselves off? These aren't plot holes—they're promises. You're telling the audience, "There's more to this story." You can ask ChatGPT for a list of small but intriguing story questions that could be teased in the background of your pilot. These moments don't require explanation right away, but they create tension and curiosity.

Don't forget your supporting characters either. They should have arcs, too—even if they're smaller or slower. A love interest, a rival, a best friend, or an antagonist can each have a trajectory that expands the world of the show. You can explore their paths with ChatGPT by asking, "What's a long-term arc for the protagonist's rival that eventually converges with the main story?" or "How could this side character become a surprise antagonist in season two?" These questions make your world feel alive, with moving parts beyond what the viewer sees right away.

And finally, tone matters. If your series arc is going to get darker, stranger, more emotional, or more epic, you can subtly reflect that trajectory in the pilot's tone. Maybe things seem light on the surface, but there's a melancholy undercurrent. Maybe the world feels stable, but the music hints at danger. These tonal shifts set expectations without giving away the game. Ask ChatGPT, "How can I foreshadow a darker second half of the season in the pilot's final scene?" and you'll get ideas for how to leave the audience with that lingering sense of "something's coming."

When done right, your pilot becomes more than just a beginning—it becomes a *launchpad*. The scenes feel tight and self-contained, but beneath them runs a current of potential. Future storylines, future reveals, future heartbreaks and victories. With ChatGPT, you can explore all those possibilities while keeping your script clean and focused. You don't need to show everything in episode one—you just need to *promise* that there's more to come.

And that promise—that quiet pull toward the horizon—is what keeps viewers coming back. Not just for the episode. But for the *journey*.

Secrets to a Memorable Climax in a Pilot

The climax of your pilot isn't just the high point of the episode—it's the moment that proves your show has legs. It's where all the tension you've been building pays off. And it's often the final impression you leave on your viewer, the thing that either makes them desperate to see episode two or ready to move on to something else. A memorable climax doesn't just wrap up the story—it cracks it open. It delivers an emotional punch, flips the stakes, or drops a reveal that changes everything. And most importantly, it sets the tone for the rest of the series. This is your chance to announce, "This is the kind of show we're going to be." With ChatGPT in your creative corner, you can shape, refine, and test your climax until it lands exactly how you want it to—with impact, clarity, and a sense of momentum.

So what actually makes a climax *memorable* in a pilot? It's not just about action or big reveals. It's about *meaning*. Something has to shift. It might be a character making a difficult choice, a new mystery being introduced, or a plan going horribly wrong. But whatever it is, it has to hit on both a plot level *and* an emotional level. The audience has to feel like something changed in a way that can't be undone. The climax of your pilot is not a resolution—it's an escalation. It's the moment where the story expands instead of closes.

One great way to approach your climax is by asking, "What is the biggest emotional question my character has been facing in this episode—and what's the moment they're forced to confront it?" Maybe they've been trying to avoid grief, and now they're finally at the funeral. Maybe they've been pretending to be someone they're not, and now the mask slips. Maybe they've been trying to keep things from falling apart, and now everything does. You can ask ChatGPT, "What's a powerful climax where this character is forced to face their greatest fear or flaw?" and you'll get scenes driven by emotional truth, not just spectacle.

Think about reversals. The best climaxes often contain a twist—a shift in power, knowledge, or stakes. Your protagonist might think they've won, only to realize they've walked into a trap. Or maybe they finally get what they want, but realize they don't want it anymore. These reversals create complexity and make the story linger in the viewer's mind. Use ChatGPT to brainstorm climactic reversals. Ask, "What's a surprising twist that could happen at the end of this episode that changes everything without feeling random?" This helps you find twists that are earned but unexpected.

If your show has a mystery element, the climax is a great place to raise a new question rather than answer an old one. Reveal just enough to keep the viewer hooked. If your show is character-driven, then the climax might be a moment of personal failure, realization, or confrontation. Either way, the climax should feel inevitable in hindsight—but surprising in the moment. Ask ChatGPT, "How can I end this pilot on a cliffhanger that feels natural and emotionally satisfying?" That will guide you toward endings that land with force and leave a door open.

Structure also matters. You don't want your climax to feel like just another scene tacked onto the end. It should feel like a culmination. You've been climbing the hill all episode—this is the peak. Usually, it comes near the end of the third act in a standard structure, or just before the final emotional beat if you're working in something more fluid. If you're unsure if your current climax is strong enough, you can say to ChatGPT, "Does this scene function well as a climax?" or "How can I raise the stakes in this moment without adding more action?" Sometimes, the issue isn't the event—it's how it's framed, how it feels.

And speaking of feelings—don't forget the emotional aftermath. A good climax should land with consequences. Even if the final scene is quiet, it should carry the weight of what just happened. A character might sit alone, wrecked by what they've done. Or they might smile, unaware of what's coming next. These final beats don't need to resolve anything, but they should *echo* the climax. Use ChatGPT to explore these reverberations: "What's a strong closing image or moment that reflects the emotional fallout of this climax?" A well-chosen ending beat can transform a good climax into a haunting one.

Visuals also play a huge role. The climax is often what the audience remembers most vividly, so think cinematically. What's the image that ends the scene? A smashed phone. An empty crib. A spilled drink. A bloodstain no one notices. These aren't just props—they're statements. Ask ChatGPT to help craft a final visual that symbolizes the shift in the story. Say, "What's a striking visual that can end this scene and suggest everything has changed?" That image is what stays in the viewer's mind—and sometimes, that's more powerful than any line of dialogue.

Also, know your genre. A climax in a thriller might be a high-stakes chase or a secret exposed. In a comedy, it might be a disaster that brings characters together. In a drama, it might be a quiet confrontation that ends a relationship or ignites a new one. Let your genre guide your pacing and tone—but don't let it limit you. Great pilots often blend expectations. You can ask ChatGPT, "What's an unexpected way to handle this climax in a romantic comedy or a sci-fi drama?" and you might find fresh takes that make your episode stand out.

Above all, your climax should make a promise. It should say, "If you stick around, this story is going to go places." It doesn't have to answer every question—it just has to make the audience *want* the answers. And it doesn't have to end with a bang—but it should end with a pull. A tug on the heart. A punch in the gut. A chill down the spine. That's the power of a well-crafted climax.

So when you sit down to write the end of your pilot, don't rush to the finish line. Ask yourself, "What's the one thing I want the viewer to feel in the final minute of this episode?" Then build the moment that delivers that feeling. And if you're not sure how to get there—ask ChatGPT. Test different versions. Explore the emotional angles. Play out the consequences.

Because when you get the climax right, the story doesn't just end—it begins again, in the mind of your audience, already wondering what happens next.

Writing the Final Scene That Leaves Them Wanting More

The final scene of your pilot is your last shot to make a first impression. It's the final emotional note, the last image the viewer sees before the screen fades to black or cuts to credits. And it's not just an ending—it's a *promise.* A signal that there's more story waiting to unfold, more secrets to uncover, more emotional arcs ready to deepen. Whether your pilot has been fast-paced or slow-burning, laugh-out-loud funny or achingly tense, the final scene needs to land in a way that makes the viewer say, "I need to see what happens next." That's not just good writing—that's good *television.* And with ChatGPT, you can refine, reshape, and rethink your final scene until it's unforgettable.

Let's start with what a great final scene *isn't.* It's not a full resolution. You're not tying up every loose end or answering every question. That might work for a short film, but not for a pilot. If everything's wrapped up, there's no reason to continue. The final scene should leave the story open—emotionally, narratively, or thematically. Something should shift, reveal itself, or crack open. Think of it as a springboard, not a landing.

One of the best strategies for a final scene is to revisit a central emotional thread—but twist it. If your protagonist has spent the episode trying to avoid confrontation, maybe the final scene forces them into one. If they've been pretending everything is fine, the final moment might be the first time we see the truth. These moments don't have to be loud—they just have to *turn.* Something has to change. You can ask ChatGPT, "What's a small but powerful shift in this character's behavior that could end the episode with emotional tension?" That one little change can do a lot of work.

Sometimes the final scene is about a reveal. A secret comes to light. A character says something they can't take back. A piece of information is discovered that reframes everything we've seen so far. This doesn't mean you need a huge plot twist—sometimes, the most powerful reveals are quiet and personal. ChatGPT can help you explore variations. Try prompts like, "Give me three possible reveals in the final scene that raise the stakes without changing the plot," or "How can I recontextualize an earlier scene with a new piece of information at the end?" These moments leave viewers leaning forward, wanting answers.

Another way to structure your final scene is around contradiction. End on a line of dialogue or an image that says one thing on the surface, but something else underneath. A character says, "I trust you," but the camera lingers on the gun hidden in their drawer. Or someone smiles and nods—just before walking away from everything. These contradictions build tension and make the world feel more complex. Ask ChatGPT, "What's a final image that contradicts a character's words or actions and adds emotional weight?" It'll help you sharpen that double meaning.

You can also go visual. Sometimes, a single striking image can say everything without dialogue. A streetlight blinking out. A couple holding hands at a crime scene. A phone ringing in an empty room. When chosen carefully, a final visual can echo your theme, tease your arc, or just leave a lingering sense of unease or curiosity. Use ChatGPT to brainstorm visuals with a prompt like, "Suggest visually evocative final moments that symbolically reflect abandonment, betrayal, or hope." These little poetic touches often stay with viewers long after the episode ends.

Another angle is to use irony. Maybe the episode ends with a character getting exactly what they wanted—only now it's the worst thing that could've happened. Or maybe someone feels victorious in a way that the audience knows is short-lived. Irony creates emotional complexity, and it's one of the sharpest tools you can use to end on a compelling note. Ask ChatGPT, "How can I use irony to close this episode in a way that adds depth to the protagonist's journey?"

And let's not forget about dialogue. Sometimes, one line is all it takes to close strong. A whispered confession. A question left hanging in the air. A seemingly throwaway remark that redefines everything. If you've built your episode with tension and subtext, your final line can land like a punch without needing to shout. You can use ChatGPT to generate alternate last lines with prompts like, "What's a final line that could end this scene on a chilling/bittersweet/hopeful note?"

The tone of your final scene should also match the emotional trajectory of your pilot. If your episode has been full of rising tension, a quiet emotional beat can feel like a perfect breath—something human after all the noise. If the episode has been slow and meditative, an abrupt moment of danger or surprise can shake things up and set the stage for a wilder season. Think of the final scene as a tone-setter for what's coming, not just a button for what came before. Use ChatGPT to check for tonal alignment by asking, "Does this final scene reflect the emotional and narrative tone of the series I'm trying to create?"

Finally, your last scene should ask a question—literally or figuratively. That question could be "What happens now?" or "Can this character recover from this?" or "Was any of that real?" If the audience walks away with a question they *want* the answer to, you've succeeded. That curiosity is the hook. You can ask ChatGPT, "What's a closing moment that leaves the viewer asking the right kind of question?" and you'll get a range of angles, from dramatic to mysterious to emotional.

The beauty of using ChatGPT is that you don't have to settle for your first idea. You can test three different endings. You can shift perspectives. You can explore how different music cues or final images change the mood. It's like having a writer's room ready to pitch twenty final scenes in five minutes.

So when you write that last page, think of it as a fuse, not a finale. Something is about to explode, unravel, bloom, or break. And your viewer? They should be right on the edge of their seat, desperate to know where it's all going.

That's when you know your final scene did its job. It didn't close the story. It *opened the door*.

Testing the Story's Logic with ChatGPT

Story logic can be a sneaky thing. When you're deep in the writing process—especially on a pilot episode—it's easy to fall in love with scenes, characters, or twists that *feel* right, but might not *make sense.* The story flows in your head, the emotional beats land, the character choices seem justified... until someone else reads it and asks, "Wait—why would they do that?" That's why it's crucial to test the internal logic of your story. Not just for plot holes or inconsistencies, but for *motivations, consequences, timing,* and *causality.* And here's the good news: ChatGPT is built for this kind of thing. It doesn't just generate new material—it can analyze what you've written and flag things that don't add up, don't track, or don't hit as hard as they should.

When we talk about story logic, we're really asking, "Does everything feel earned?" That means character choices need to align with who they are. Cause needs to lead to effect. Secrets need to be kept for believable reasons. Coincidences need to be rare or justified. If something shocking happens in your story, it better either be well foreshadowed or feel thematically correct. And if a character makes a major decision, it has to feel emotionally honest—even if it's irrational, it must be irrational in a way *we believe.* These are the kinds of things ChatGPT can help you pressure test.

Let's say you've written a scene where your protagonist turns down a major opportunity—something they've supposedly been fighting for all episode. You can paste the scene into ChatGPT and ask, "Does this decision make sense based on everything the character has said and done so far?" The AI can give you an outside-eye perspective, pointing out whether the moment feels consistent or arbitrary. It might suggest you add a line of internal conflict earlier, or reveal a piece of backstory that justifies the choice. That way, the decision feels like part of an emotional arc—not a plot twist forced in for drama.

You can also use ChatGPT to check the sequence of events. Ask it, "Does this scene logically follow the one before it?" or "Is there a clearer way for this information to come out?" It might point out a time jump that feels confusing, or a missing beat that would help bridge two emotional moments. It's like having a script supervisor who never sleeps.

One of the most powerful things you can do is run a "cause and effect" test. Paste a few key plot points and ask ChatGPT, "Does every major event have a clear cause and a believable effect?" If something just *happens* without reason—like a character suddenly changing their mind or an antagonist showing up at the exact right time—you might need to go back and thread it better. The goal isn't to remove all surprise, but to make sure the surprise feels earned. You want your viewer to think, "I didn't see that coming, but of course it had to happen."

Logic checks are also useful for character relationships. Ask ChatGPT, "Do the interactions between these two characters evolve in a believable way across the episode?" If the chemistry feels rushed, or a betrayal doesn't land because there's no setup, the AI can help you identify where to build more tension or intimacy. You don't always need to rewrite the scenes—you might just need to rearrange them, add a beat of silence, or change a line of dialogue. ChatGPT can suggest micro-adjustments that strengthen the emotional logic.

If your story includes world-building—especially in science fiction, fantasy, or high-concept drama—logic becomes even more important. Rules need to be consistent. If a character can teleport in scene five, the audience will wonder why they didn't teleport to escape danger in scene eight. Use ChatGPT to test your world's internal consistency: "Based on these rules, are there any plot problems in this episode?" or "What are the potential logical gaps in how this technology or system works?" It can flag loopholes you might not have spotted because you're so close to the material.

You can even ask ChatGPT to play devil's advocate. Say, "Pretend you're a critical viewer poking holes in this story. What might you question or challenge?" It'll give you an honest breakdown of anything that feels too convenient, underdeveloped, or contradictory. And because it's not emotionally attached to your scenes, it won't hesitate to point out the weak spots. That's incredibly valuable—especially before handing your pilot off to producers, agents, or showrunners who *will* ask those tough questions.

Another great use of ChatGPT is to test what *isn't* on the page. Say you've written a confrontation scene between two characters, and you think it works. But when you ask ChatGPT, "What is the audience likely to assume about this character's motives based on this scene?" the answer might surprise you. Maybe the dialogue accidentally makes the character seem more manipulative or less sympathetic than you intended. Maybe their actions suggest a deeper motive you haven't explored yet. These insights can help you clarify your intent and make sure the emotional subtext is coming through as planned.

You can also test pacing logic. If something happens too quickly—or takes too long—your story can lose tension or credibility. Ask ChatGPT, "Does this reveal come too early or too late?" or "What needs to happen between these scenes to make this transition feel earned?" It might suggest a shorter lead-in, a moment of hesitation, or a breadcrumb planted earlier. These tweaks can keep your story flowing without rushing or dragging.

Even minor details can have major effects. If your pilot has a subplot involving, say, a hidden affair or a missing item, you can ask ChatGPT, "Are there any inconsistencies in how this subplot is presented?" or "Does the resolution of this thread make narrative sense?" The AI might catch a missing setup, a timeline glitch, or an unclear motivation—and offer fixes that don't require overhauling the whole script.

And sometimes, the best thing ChatGPT can do is ask *you* the right questions. You might get a reply like, "What is the character afraid will happen if they tell the truth in this scene?" or "Why would the antagonist choose this moment to strike?" These questions push you to think more deeply about your story's logic—not in a mechanical way, but in an emotionally and thematically cohesive way.

So before you lock your script and hit export, take a beat to run it through a logic check. Use ChatGPT like a story mechanic—tightening loose bolts, checking under the hood, making sure the engine actually runs. It doesn't have to be perfect. But it *does* need to feel real. Honest. Believable within its own world.

Because when the logic is strong, the viewer stops questioning—and starts feeling. And that's where the magic really begins.

Writing Descriptive Action without Slowing the Story

Writing action in a pilot script is like walking a tightrope. You need to be vivid and cinematic so the reader can *see* what's happening, but you also need to keep the pace moving so the story doesn't feel like it's stuck in slow motion. The biggest mistake writers make is overloading action lines with too much detail, bogging down the rhythm of the scene and pulling focus away from the momentum. On the flip side, some writers go too lean—writing flat, generic action that leaves the scene feeling empty. The sweet spot is writing action that's descriptive *and* dynamic, visual *and* efficient. It should be specific, sharp, and always in service of story or character. And with ChatGPT, you can experiment with different levels of description until you find that balance that reads fast and plays even faster in the mind's eye.

Let's start with the purpose of action in a pilot. It's not just about choreography. It's about tone. It's about building tension, revealing emotion, showing the world in motion, and keeping the energy up between dialogue beats. Whether it's someone storming into a room, packing a suitcase in silence, or dodging bullets across rooftops, the action should *do* something narratively or emotionally. That's why every movement you describe should feel intentional, not ornamental. You can ask ChatGPT, "How can I rewrite this action to reflect the character's inner state?" and suddenly the physicality becomes storytelling.

One of the key techniques is writing in *present tense* with *short, punchy sentences*. Action shouldn't feel literary—it should feel like watching a movie. Instead of "He slowly walks through the corridor, glancing nervously at each doorway," try "He walks. Slow. Checking each door. Every creak makes him flinch." These staccato beats build suspense and pull the reader into the scene moment by moment. You can use ChatGPT to help tighten long action paragraphs. Just paste it in and ask, "Make this more cinematic and concise." You'll get a version that trims the fat and adds edge.

Avoid over-directing. You don't need to list every physical movement unless it's critical to the story. Focus on *key beats*—the ones that change the energy in the room or escalate the tension. If someone throws a punch, describe the *feel* of the moment, not just the mechanics. You can write, "He swings wild, desperate—connects. Bone cracks. She stumbles back, eyes wide." It's not just a fight—it's a power shift. Use ChatGPT to find that emotional layer. Try asking, "How can I describe this action beat to show rising panic?" or "What physical detail would make this feel more personal?"

Another smart tactic is to *suggest* rather than *explain*. You don't need to describe every object in the room unless it's important. Instead of "A vintage leather couch with ornate wooden legs sits in the middle of the room," just say, "A battered leather couch, like it's seen too many confessions." One line, and we get it. You can ask ChatGPT, "How can I suggest atmosphere with a few sharp visual details?" and you'll get sensory cues that give the scene texture without slowing it down.

Movement should match pacing. Fast action reads fast. Short lines. Sharp turns. Slow scenes need rhythm, weight, and silence. Let the reader *feel* the tempo in the way you format the scene. Use line breaks to control pacing. For example:

He stares at the door.

Then opens it.

And everything changes.

Each line creates a beat. A pause. A shift. These visual cues on the page affect how the scene is read and imagined. ChatGPT can help you rewrite action using rhythm. Ask, "Can you give this scene a pacing that builds dread?" or "Rewrite this beat with more urgency, using shorter sentence structure." The difference is immediate.

Use action to reveal character. Someone slamming a door isn't just angry—it might be the first time they've let themselves feel anything in days. A person cleaning obsessively while others argue might not care about the fight—they care about control. These subtle behaviors say more than dialogue sometimes. If you have a scene with dialogue and need physical behavior that matches (or subverts) emotion, ask ChatGPT, "What physical actions might a character do while hiding their anxiety in this scene?" You'll get real, character-driven gestures that deepen the moment.

When writing ensemble scenes or chaotic sequences, clarity is your friend. Don't try to cram too much into one block of action. Separate beats. Make sure we know who's doing what and why it matters. In action-heavy pilots—thrillers, procedurals, sci-fi—you need to balance spectacle with readability. Ask ChatGPT to help streamline: "Simplify this action sequence without losing impact," or "Break this chaotic scene into clear beats with distinct emotional shifts." It'll help you organize the moment so it plays with precision.

Transitions are another underrated area for action writing. Don't just jump from location to location—use visual transitions that carry emotion or suggest story. Someone walking out of a hospital into bright daylight. A train door closing. A cigarette smouldering in an ashtray. These visual buttons and scene entries build a flow that keeps the story moving. Ask ChatGPT, "What's a visual action that could transition this scene into the next with tension intact?" and you'll get clever, cinematic bridges.

And remember, sometimes the most powerful action is *stillness*. A character frozen in place. A tear held back. A moment where everything stops. These beats are just as visual, just as emotional, and often more memorable than explosions or chase scenes. Use ChatGPT to help write moments of silent impact. Try, "How can I show heartbreak in a quiet visual moment?" and you'll get options that break hearts with no words at all.

Descriptive action isn't about writing more—it's about writing *better*. Sharper. Smarter. More cinematic. With ChatGPT, you can run scene after scene, testing tone, pacing, clarity, and visual detail until your pages feel alive. You're not just writing a pilot—you're crafting a *show*. One that plays in the reader's imagination as clearly as it will on screen.

So as you work through your script, keep this in mind: action isn't just motion. It's story, tone, and character, moving in real time. And when written with precision and flair, it doesn't slow the story down—it *drives it forward*.

Crafting High Stakes that Matter

High stakes are the fuel that powers your pilot. They're what keep the audience locked in, what make your characters' decisions feel urgent, and what give weight to every scene. Without real stakes, the story drifts. With them, every choice has consequences, every moment matters, and the viewer leans in because they *care*. But stakes aren't just about world-ending scenarios or life-or-death situations. They're about what your characters stand to lose—or gain—and how much it *matters* to them personally. The trick is to make the stakes feel intimate, emotional, and specific. And when you're using ChatGPT, you can test those stakes from every angle, making sure they hold up not just on paper, but in the hearts and minds of your characters and audience.

Let's start with what stakes *really* are. They're the cost of failure. If your character doesn't get what they want, what happens? What do they lose? What falls apart? The more that answer matters to your character, the more we care too. It could be something big—like losing a job, a home, a child. But it could also be something small that *feels* big—like losing self-respect, a friendship, or a shot at redemption. The key isn't size—it's *weight*. Ask ChatGPT, "What's a personal cost this character might face if they fail at their goal?" You'll get answers rooted in emotion, which always hits harder than vague consequences.

One way to raise stakes is to make the goal deeply personal. If your protagonist is trying to solve a crime, that's interesting. If they're trying to solve the crime that got their sister killed and they're hiding the fact that they saw it happen, now it's *charged*. The stakes aren't just justice—they're guilt, truth, exposure, grief. You can ask ChatGPT, "How can I raise the emotional stakes of this plot without changing the core story?" and it'll show you ways to embed meaning inside the mission.

Another powerful move is to *double up* your stakes. Make your character fight on two fronts—internal and external. Maybe they're trying to win a court case, but if they win, they'll have to betray a close friend. Now the story is no longer about right vs. wrong—it's about what kind of person they want to be. You can prompt ChatGPT, "What's a dilemma that could turn this simple goal into a moral or emotional conflict?" and watch the story grow deeper and more intense.

Stakes also rise when there's *pressure*. A time limit. A rival. A secret that could be revealed. These elements tighten the noose around your character. They can't just wander toward their goal—they're being pushed, cornered, squeezed. Add urgency. ChatGPT can help create pressure by answering, "What ticking clock could be introduced to increase tension in this pilot?" or "What external force could raise the risk of failure for this character?" Now your pilot has momentum.

One underrated way to make stakes matter is to show us what happens *if they succeed*. Not all success is good. Maybe your protagonist gets the promotion but becomes the kind of person they used to hate. Maybe they get revenge and realize they've become just like the person they were trying to destroy. Ask ChatGPT, "What's a consequence of winning that would complicate the protagonist's arc?" It'll help you turn even victories into questions—and keep the tension going past the end of the pilot.

Stakes can also be *symbolic*. Maybe your story is about a boxer trying to win a fight—but the fight is also about reclaiming his father's legacy. Or a teenager trying to get into college—but what she really wants is freedom from a suffocating home life. The surface stakes and the deeper stakes are connected, but it's the deeper ones that *stick*. Ask ChatGPT to help you uncover them: "What's the emotional or symbolic meaning behind this goal?" and your story will gain an added layer of resonance.

Relationships are a great tool for amplifying stakes. A choice that affects someone your protagonist loves—or could lose—will always land harder. Maybe they're chasing a dream, but doing so might mean leaving behind the person who supported them from day one. Or maybe they're trying to protect someone who doesn't even know they're in danger. The more relationships are tested, the higher the emotional cost of failure. Ask ChatGPT, "How can this plot challenge or threaten a key relationship in the story?" and it'll help you find new ways to twist the knife.

Don't forget that *revealing* stakes can be just as powerful as raising them. Maybe the character doesn't even know what's truly at risk until halfway through the pilot. A twist of knowledge can shift the entire meaning of the story. What seemed like a simple task suddenly has personal or political consequences. You can use ChatGPT to map this out: "What's a twist that changes the character's understanding of what's at stake?" This type of late reveal can re-energize the back half of your pilot.

And finally, stakes are only as good as the *buy-in* from your character. If they don't seem to care, neither will we. That doesn't mean they have to cry or shout. But they do need to *act*. To fight, to sacrifice, to risk. Show us that the goal matters to them—and that the cost is real. If you're not sure it's coming through, ask ChatGPT, "How can I show that this goal truly matters to my character without making them say it?" You'll get action-based, behavior-driven ideas that make the stakes feel earned and immediate.

Great stakes aren't about explosions or death. They're about meaning. They're about what the character values—and what it will do to them if they lose it. They give your pilot weight, drive your structure, fuel your conflict, and hook your audience emotionally.

And with ChatGPT helping you pressure test every scene, every choice, every moment—you're not just writing *a* story. You're writing *one that matters*. To the characters. To the viewers. And to you.

Balancing Exposition with Engagement

Exposition is a necessary evil—or at least, that's how a lot of writers see it. In a pilot, there's so much the audience needs to understand: who the characters are, what their relationships are, what the world is like, what's already happened, and what's at stake moving forward. That's a tall order, especially when you've also got to keep things emotionally compelling, visually dynamic, and tonally consistent. But here's the good news: exposition doesn't have to be a drag. In fact, when it's handled right, exposition becomes invisible. It folds into the dialogue, the action, and the emotional beats so naturally that the audience absorbs it without even realizing it. The trick is balance—knowing how to feed information without stopping the story. And with ChatGPT as your creative partner, you can stress-test your exposition and find fresh, engaging ways to deliver it that keep the viewer glued to every scene.

The first thing to understand is that *when* you deliver information is just as important as *how*. A common mistake in pilots is front-loading everything. Writers often try to explain the entire world and all the character dynamics in the first five pages, which almost always slows down the pacing and weakens the hook. If the audience is spending the opening scenes mentally cataloging facts, they're not emotionally connecting. That's the danger. You don't need to explain everything upfront. You just need to explain *enough* for the audience to want to know more.

Ask yourself: What *must* the audience know to understand and feel this scene? Then only include that. Anything else can wait. You can ask ChatGPT, "What's the minimum amount of information I need to include in this scene for it to make sense?" and it'll help you trim the fat while keeping the story clear. This helps you drip-feed the information over time, so the viewer is always learning—but never overloaded.

One of the best ways to deliver exposition is through *conflict*. When characters are arguing, defending themselves, or trying to hide something, they reveal information in ways that feel natural and charged. Instead of saying, "You know I haven't spoken to Dad since he remarried," make it a fight: "Oh, now you want to talk about family? Where were you when he married her?" That line gives us the same information, but wrapped in emotional tension. ChatGPT can help you reframe flat exposition into conflict-driven dialogue. Just say, "Turn this exposition into a tense argument," and watch how quickly it becomes something you'd actually want to watch.

Another trick is to bury exposition in behavior. People show what they know or believe by how they act. A character who triple-checks locks might have a history of trauma. Someone who avoids elevators might have survived a collapse. You don't need to *say* these things. You show them. Ask ChatGPT, "What behaviors might hint at this character's backstory without dialogue?" and it'll help you communicate important information visually and sub-textually, which is pure gold in a screenplay.

You can also let your *world* do some of the exposition work. If your show takes place in a futuristic city, a character casually scanning their palm to enter a building tells us something about the technology and the society—no one needs to explain how the scanner works. Environmental exposition is often the most elegant. Ask ChatGPT, "How can I show the economic class divide in this world without dialogue?" and you'll get ideas for settings, props, and background action that do the heavy lifting for you.

And then there's the art of implication. Instead of outright telling the audience that a character has a secret, let them *suspect* it. Let the audience do some of the work. It makes them feel smart, and it makes your writing more layered. A silence that lingers too long. A glance that doesn't match the words. A door that's locked when it shouldn't be.

ChatGPT is great at finding these subtle touches—try, "How can I imply this secret without stating it?" and you'll get suggestions that keep things engaging and mysterious.

Voiceover is another exposition tool, but it's dangerous. When used well, it adds style, character, and clarity. When used poorly, it feels like a crutch. If you're considering voiceover, ask ChatGPT to help you write a version of the scene with and without it. Compare the impact. Sometimes, just turning the voiceover into internal dialogue or reworking the visual storytelling gets you to the same place more effectively.

Montages, flashbacks, news reports, overheard conversations, even comedy bits—there are endless ways to hide exposition in plain sight. If you're stuck, give ChatGPT your scene and ask, "What are five creative ways to deliver this information without traditional exposition?" You might end up with a phone call, a visual clue, a recurring joke, or a silent moment that says everything.

But here's the real secret: exposition works best when it *creates curiosity*. Don't answer every question—plant them. Let the viewer wonder. If you tell us the protagonist is estranged from their brother, okay. But if you *show* them ignoring a call from someone labeled "Don't Answer (David)," we're *interested*. We want to know why. That curiosity pulls the audience forward. Use ChatGPT to test your exposition for mystery. Ask, "Does this line spark curiosity or shut it down?" If it doesn't spark something, it might need a rewrite.

You can even ask ChatGPT to run an exposition audit. Paste a scene and say, "What exposition in this scene could be shown rather than told?" or "Which lines feel like information dumps instead of story?" It'll break it down and offer cleaner alternatives, giving you a sharper, more dynamic version of your scene.

At the end of the day, balancing exposition with engagement is about trust. Trust the audience to pick things up. Trust the visuals to carry some of the weight. Trust your characters to reveal themselves through action, behavior, and emotion. And trust yourself to know when enough is enough.

Because when exposition flows with energy, subtlety, and intent—your world comes alive. And the audience doesn't just *understand* your story. They *feel* it. And that's the real goal.

How to Create a Pilot with Re-watch Value

When you think about your favorite TV pilots—the ones you return to again and again—they tend to have one thing in common: layers. Every time you watch them, you notice something new. A line that hinted at a future twist. A character detail you didn't appreciate the first time around. A bit of dialogue that hits harder once you know where the story goes. That's what gives a pilot *rewatch value*. It's not just about crafting a solid first-time viewing experience; it's about building something rich enough to reward a second look—and maybe even a third. The best pilots aren't just introductions; they're blueprints for the series, loaded with intentional choices that echo far beyond the opening hour. And the good news is, you don't have to build all those layers alone—ChatGPT can help you load your script with subtle setups, smart symbolism, and narrative echoes that make your pilot worth revisiting.

Rewatch value begins with *foreshadowing*. When you know where your series is headed—even just in broad strokes—you can plant small hints throughout the pilot that will make future developments feel earned. These might be lines of dialogue, specific props, recurring imagery, or character choices that only make sense in hindsight. The key is subtlety. You don't want the audience to notice them the first time—but you want them to feel a little shiver of recognition when they see it again. You can ask ChatGPT, "What kind of foreshadowing can I include in this scene to hint at a later betrayal?" or "What's a symbolic object I can introduce now that will pay off later in the season?" These details don't just add texture—they turn viewers into detectives, eager to connect the dots.

Another ingredient of re-watch value is *theme*. If your pilot has a strong thematic core—an emotional idea or philosophical question—it becomes easier to create moments that resonate on multiple levels. For example, if your theme is about identity, then every interaction, every bit of conflict, and every visual detail can reflect some aspect of that struggle. The viewer might not consciously clock it the first time, but on re-watch, they'll see how tightly woven everything is. Ask ChatGPT, "How can I reinforce the theme of 'control vs. chaos' through character actions in this scene?" and you'll get ideas that deepen the impact of every beat.

Re-watchable pilots also tend to feature *character-driven mysteries*. These don't have to be plot mysteries, like a murder or a missing person. They can be emotional or psychological mysteries. Why does this character act this way? What are they hiding? What happened in their past that makes them tick like this? When viewers go back, they want to trace those motivations and see how early signs were there all along. You can use ChatGPT to help layer these mysteries. Try, "What are some subtle ways I can hint that this character isn't telling the whole truth?" or "How can I make this side character seem harmless now, but suspicious in retrospect?"

Another aspect of a great re-watch is *parallelism*. That's when you create echoes across your story that become clearer on multiple viewings. Maybe a line of dialogue in the pilot mirrors something said in the finale. Maybe a location we see in episode one becomes crucial later. These structural patterns add richness and make the story feel carefully constructed. ChatGPT can help you build these connections by asking, "What kind of scene could mirror this one later in the series for emotional impact?" or "How can I set up a visual motif that evolves over time?"

You also boost re-watch value by crafting *multi-dimensional dialogue*. A great line can carry surface meaning, subtext, and foreshadowing all at once. Maybe a character says something sarcastic that feels like a joke—until you realize on re-watch that it was true. Or maybe two characters banter playfully, but their body language tells a very different story. You can work with ChatGPT to refine dialogue for layered meaning. Ask, "Can you rewrite this line so it works as both a joke and a subtle threat?" or "How can I make this exchange feel flirty now but sinister later?"

Let's not forget *visual re-watchability*. The images you put on screen can carry hidden meaning, metaphors, or callbacks. A painting in the background. A piece of clothing. The way a scene is framed. These visuals can quietly communicate more than the dialogue and can take on new meaning when you know what's coming. Ask ChatGPT, "What's a visual metaphor I can include in this scene that foreshadows loss?" or "How can I use lighting or space to reflect a character's emotional state?" Even in the script phase, you're directing a mental movie—and planting the visuals now gives your show layers later.

Subplots and side characters can also add re-watchability—especially if they're not fully explained at first. Maybe a background character behaves oddly in a way that's brushed off, but on rewatch, you realize they were the key to everything. Or a subplot feels like comic relief, but later ties into the main story in a huge way. You can ask ChatGPT, "What's a subplot that seems minor now but could take on greater meaning later in the series?" This kind of storytelling rewards close attention and invites viewers back for clues they missed.

Finally, pacing plays a part in re-watch value. A tightly structured pilot with moments of breathing room gives viewers space to notice things. If your script is too fast, all the nuance gets steamrolled. If it's too slow, the audience won't make it to the second watch. With ChatGPT, you can test the rhythm of your scenes. Try, "Can you add a subtle emotional beat to this fast-paced scene without slowing it down too much?" or "What's a quiet moment I can insert that deepens character and adds rewatch value?" These kinds of moments make the world feel lived-in—and worth returning to.

Ultimately, re-watch value comes from *intention*. From knowing what your story is really about and planting those meanings in every frame, every line, and every choice. With ChatGPT helping you dig deeper, refine the layers, and test every detail, you don't just write a good pilot—you build a world that invites people back.

Because that's the magic of television. Not just getting viewers to hit play—but making them hit it *again*.

Writing for a Binge-Watching Audience

Binge-watching has changed the way people watch television—and that means it has also changed how we write it. Gone are the days when a pilot had to serve mainly as a standalone pitch to network executives or hook viewers who'd wait a week for the next episode. Today, if your show is on a streaming platform, there's a good chance your pilot will be watched *immediately* before the next episode. That shift in viewing habits changes how pilots work. They don't need to wrap things up. They need to *launch* things. For a binge-watching audience, a pilot isn't just an opener—it's episode one of a long, addictive experience. And your job is to write it in a way that makes it impossible not to keep watching. With ChatGPT by your side, you can structure, pace, and craft your pilot to serve that modern storytelling rhythm from page one.

So what makes writing for a binge-watching audience different? First, there's the matter of *momentum*. A binge-worthy pilot needs to move. It needs to keep tension alive, escalate conflict, and layer in mysteries that can't possibly be resolved in forty-five minutes. The audience doesn't need everything tied up—they need something *opened*. That means the plot should end in motion. The character arcs should feel like they're just beginning. And the final moments should contain a clear emotional or narrative *pull* into episode two. You can ask ChatGPT, "What's a closing beat that launches the next episode emotionally?" or "What's a moment that ends on rising tension instead of resolution?" That way, your pilot ends like a spring—loaded with potential energy.

Another key element is *interconnected storytelling*. In binge-era shows, there's less pressure to make each episode standalone. That gives you freedom to thread stories across episodes, to leave questions unanswered, and to build arcs that simmer slowly. Still, that doesn't mean your pilot can drift or meander. It needs a strong engine. The audience should finish the episode knowing who the show is about, what they're up against, and why it matters. The *what comes next* should be baked into the final scenes. Ask ChatGPT, "What new problem or complication could naturally emerge in the last scene of my pilot to pull us into episode two?" and you'll find ways to carry your momentum into the next hour without needing a forced cliffhanger.

Character is crucial. Binge-watching is a relationship. Viewers are investing several hours (sometimes an entire weekend) with your characters, so the pilot needs to create emotional bonds right away. That doesn't mean your characters need to be likable, but they *do* need to be intriguing. We need to understand what drives them—even if we don't understand everything about them yet. Use ChatGPT to stress-test your character intros: "How can I make this character's introduction more emotionally compelling?" or "What's a scene that hints at deeper complexity without explaining everything?" That mystery is what keeps viewers leaning in.

Pacing is also different in binge-style storytelling. You don't want to blow all your big reveals or twists too early, but you also can't take five episodes to get interesting. Your pilot needs to feel like a *promise*—one that says, "Stick around. You're going to love where this goes." The best pilots for binge-watching plant multiple questions and start answering *just* enough of them to build trust. That sense of trust is what gets a viewer to hit "Next Episode." Ask ChatGPT, "What questions am I raising in this pilot, and which ones should I delay answering to increase suspense?" It helps you design a flow of tension and payoff that stretches across multiple episodes.

Dialogue and scene construction matter more than ever. In binge-friendly TV, dialogue often does double duty: it advances plot, reveals character, and delivers theme in compact, memorable bursts. Scenes don't linger longer than they need to. They cut in late, get to the point, and end on a turn or revelation. You can use ChatGPT to tighten your script by asking, "Trim this scene to the essential emotional and narrative beats," or "What's a sharper version of this dialogue that hits harder without extra words?" These little improvements keep the story flowing fast and clean—perfect for binge-style pacing.

Tone is also a big factor. Binge-watchers want consistency—but they also crave variety within that consistency. If your pilot is all grim all the time, it can be exhausting. If it's all jokes, it can start to feel shallow. A bingeable pilot blends tones—comedy inside drama, suspense inside stillness, heartache right after laughter. This keeps viewers emotionally invested. You can use ChatGPT to play with tonal shifts. Ask, "Where could I add a surprising emotional beat in this scene?" or "What's a moment of levity that doesn't undercut the tension?" These tonal pivots are what make long sessions of watching feel emotionally textured rather than flat.

Structure still matters—especially if you're thinking about arcs. Even if the first episode is meant to lead directly into the next, it should still feel like a *unit*. That means giving it a shape. A beginning, middle, and end—even if that "end" opens a new door instead of closing the last one. You can outline your structure with ChatGPT's help. Try, "Give me a three-act breakdown for a binge-friendly pilot," or "What's a midpoint twist that could reframe the protagonist's goal?" You're still telling a complete story, even if it's just act one of a larger experience.

Music, rhythm, and energy also play a bigger role when viewers are watching multiple episodes in a row. The tone of your final moments affects how people *feel* about the entire hour. A pilot that ends in a whisper after a slow build might not feel like enough—even if it's brilliant. You want to leave them wanting more. Use ChatGPT to brainstorm endings that have forward thrust: "What's a final moment that leaves a viewer emotionally unsettled or intrigued?" or "What's a beat that launches a new conflict right as the credits roll?"

And don't be afraid to let things *breathe* when it counts. Binge audiences actually enjoy moments of stillness—as long as the emotional tension is high. A quiet character beat, a haunting visual, a loaded silence between two people—that's the kind of moment people remember when they hit pause, even after hours of viewing. Ask ChatGPT, "What's a silent moment that could carry emotional weight at the end of this scene?" and it'll help you find those tiny gems that linger in the viewer's memory.

Ultimately, writing for a binge-watching audience is about momentum, emotion, and layering. You're not just creating one great episode—you're creating an *invitation*. A door into a story that promises depth, surprise, evolution, and meaning. And with ChatGPT, you can build and refine that invitation scene by scene, line by line, until it's irresistible.

Because in the world of streaming, there's no better compliment than someone hitting "Next Episode" before the credits finish rolling. And that starts with the kind of pilot they can't walk away from.

Using Repetition and Callbacks to Reinforce Themes

One of the most powerful ways to make your pilot feel cohesive, resonant, and emotionally grounded is through repetition and callbacks. These are the subtle tools that give a script that sense of rhythm and payoff—that feeling that everything is connected, nothing is random, and the writer knows exactly what they're doing. Repetition doesn't mean hitting the audience over the head with the same information—it means weaving a concept, phrase, image, or action through your script in a way that reinforces your theme without being obvious. Callbacks are your echoes. They're the moments where something earlier in the story comes back—twisted, reframed, or deepened—and suddenly it hits differently. And both of these tools are incredibly effective when you're building a story around a central theme. They turn ideas into patterns. They make themes feel lived-in. And with ChatGPT helping you brainstorm and track them, you can build a pilot that feels thoughtful, layered, and emotionally sticky.

Let's start with repetition. This can be a phrase a character keeps saying. A piece of visual imagery. A situation that keeps reoccurring in different forms. What makes repetition effective is when it's intentional. If your theme is about control, for example, you might show different characters trying to control their surroundings—locking doors, adjusting their outfits, micromanaging others. These actions, spread throughout the pilot, start to signal a larger emotional truth without a single line of exposition. You can ask ChatGPT, "What's a behavior I can repeat across characters to reinforce the theme of control?" and suddenly you're building a motif that runs quietly but powerfully in the background of your scenes.

Repetition in dialogue is another strong tactic. A phrase that means one thing early on and something completely different by the end of the episode has emotional punch. A mother might say to her child, "You'll understand when you're older," early in the story—and later, that child might repeat it to someone else in a moment of disillusionment. That's not just a callback. That's evolution. You can use ChatGPT to generate phrases that hold multiple meanings. Ask, "What's a line that could feel comforting at first but ominous later?" and you'll get language that's loaded with thematic potential.

Callbacks are all about payoff. Something introduced early comes back later, ideally with more weight. This doesn't always have to be plot-driven. Sometimes it's emotional. A character who refuses to dance in an early scene might finally do so in a private, broken moment—that's a callback. A joke that seemed harmless becomes devastating when it resurfaces. An object we saw in passing becomes crucial later. These moments are satisfying because they reward the viewer's attention. They say, "This story remembers." You can use ChatGPT to map these moments. Ask, "What's a setup in the first ten pages that could pay off in the final scene?" and it will help you build structure through reflection.

One great method is to mirror scenes. Let two scenes play out with similar structure or framing—but change the context. A character might have a breakfast scene in the beginning where they're relaxed and happy, and another one at the end where they're completely broken—but the location and rhythm are the same. That mirrored structure reinforces how far they've come, and what the story has done to them. Ask ChatGPT, "How can I mirror this scene later in the episode to reflect the character's emotional transformation?" and you'll be surprised how much weight repetition can carry without a single line of added dialogue.

Symbolism also benefits from repetition. If you associate a symbol—like water, fire, birds, mirrors—with your theme, you can return to it throughout the pilot. Maybe every time your character lies, they see their reflection. Maybe fire appears in moments of emotional rupture. You're not just repeating an image—you're reinforcing an idea through sensory storytelling. ChatGPT can help you come up with those symbols. Try, "What visual symbols represent inner conflict that I can repeat subtly through the script?" and you'll start building a visual vocabulary for your story.

Repetition and callbacks also help build your story's *music*. Just like a song has verses and choruses, your script can have moments that echo, return, or evolve. It makes the story feel more intentional and emotionally complete. These rhythmic choices matter, especially in a pilot, because they set the tone for how the rest of the series will function. You're teaching your audience how to watch your show—what to notice, what to expect, and how to connect the dots. ChatGPT can help refine this with prompts like, "Identify three story beats that could be echoed later for emotional payoff," or "Find places in the script to repeat a visual idea in a new context."

One important note: the key to successful repetition is change. If you repeat something exactly the same way every time, it becomes static. But if you repeat it with variation—if it evolves—it becomes meaningful. A character repeating a joke from episode one in episode six might feel nostalgic, or heartbreaking, or ironic, depending on what's changed. That shift is where the power lives. Ask ChatGPT, "How can I repeat this moment later in the story to show how everything has changed?" and you'll be layering story and character development into the bones of your script.

Even small callbacks can have big impact. A look. A gesture. A ringtone. A song. A choice reversed. These little echoes create emotional continuity. They create moments of recognition that hit the viewer in the gut. And they make your story feel whole. Not just something happening *now*, but something that remembers where it's been.

So when you write your pilot, don't just move forward—loop back. Echo. Reflect. Repeat. Let your characters revisit their own patterns. Let your audience hear the rhythm. Let the theme grow louder every time it returns.

Because when you use repetition and callbacks with intention, your story stops being a series of events—and starts being a symphony. And that's what keeps people coming back, episode after episode, again and again.

How ChatGPT Helps You Think Like a Showrunner

Writing a pilot isn't just about crafting a great first episode—it's about proving you can command an entire series. That's the showrunner's mindset. It's thinking not just like a writer, but like the creative architect of a world, the conductor of multiple storylines, the keeper of tone, character, pacing, and theme. Most writers focus on the page. Showrunners focus on the big picture. And the beautiful thing about using ChatGPT while writing your pilot is that it doesn't just help you with lines of dialogue or scene descriptions—it helps you *think bigger*. It pushes you to step into the role of the storyteller-in-chief, which is exactly the mindset you need to build something lasting, layered, and binge-worthy.

The first way ChatGPT helps you think like a showrunner is by helping you build out the *entire world*. You might have a great protagonist and a killer hook, but a showrunner looks beyond that and asks, "What's happening just outside the frame?" With ChatGPT, you can explore the corners of your world without writing endless exposition. You can say, "What are five background details I can include to suggest this city is falling apart economically?" or "What's the history of this town that influences how these characters behave?" Suddenly, you're not just writing a script—you're creating a place that lives and breathes beyond the scenes.

Then there's your *character bench*. A showrunner doesn't just focus on the lead—they think about the ensemble, the character arcs that could run for seasons, the side players who will eventually step into the spotlight. ChatGPT can help you map those long-term arcs. Ask, "Where could this supporting character go emotionally by season two?" or "How might this character grow or break down over five episodes?" When you start thinking in terms of character evolution and intersecting storylines, you're already shifting from screenwriter to showrunner.

A showrunner also sees *theme* as more than just subtext—it's the engine that drives choices, conflict, and design. ChatGPT can help you clarify your theme, then thread it through the entire script. Say, "The theme of my show is the illusion of control—how can I reflect that in character, visuals, and dialogue?" You'll get specific ideas that make your script feel cohesive and intentional. Showrunners don't just want a good scene—they want every scene to say something about the big idea.

Structure is another big one. Showrunners think in arcs—episode arcs, season arcs, series arcs. If your pilot is the seed, the showrunner is already thinking about the tree. Where does this story *want* to go? What's the midpoint of season one? What secret is going to unravel by episode six? With ChatGPT, you can test these ideas before you even finish the pilot. Try, "What's a five-episode structure for this storyline that escalates tension and develops characters?" or "How can I introduce a mystery in the pilot that slowly unfolds across the season?" This level of planning doesn't just help you pitch better—it makes your writing stronger right now.

Tone is another thing that separates writers from showrunners. It's not just about what's said—it's about how it *feels*. A showrunner keeps the tone consistent and intentional across every episode. ChatGPT can help you test for tonal balance. Ask, "Does this scene match the overall tone of a grounded sci-fi drama?" or "How can I adjust this dialogue to fit a dark comedy without losing meaning?" You're no longer just writing—you're directing the vibe of the whole show.

Showrunners also need to think about *repetition, callbacks, and continuity*—the stuff that gives a show depth. With ChatGPT, you can ask, "What lines from this pilot could come back in later episodes for emotional or thematic payoff?" or "How can I turn this character quirk into a recurring device?" These kinds of details turn a script into a universe.

Even logistics—yes, the boring stuff—are part of the showrunner mindset. Budget, locations, cast size, feasibility. Writing with production in mind makes your pilot more viable. If you're writing for a streaming-style show, ChatGPT can help you adapt accordingly. Ask, "How can I stage this scene with minimal locations and still keep it visually interesting?" or "What are ways to suggest a larger world without expensive set pieces?" Suddenly, you're thinking like someone who knows how to *make* the show, not just write it.

And of course, the best showrunners don't do it alone. They build a team, a room, a process. ChatGPT becomes your first room of one. You can bounce ideas around, test scenes, ask for feedback, play out alternate versions. "What if the protagonist made the opposite choice in this scene?" or "What's a more subtle way to reveal this backstory?" That back-and-forth, that ability to explore dozens of possibilities in minutes, mirrors what a showrunner does every day in a writers' room.

In the end, thinking like a showrunner means thinking beyond the script. It means seeing the bigger shape of the story, planning the emotional architecture of seasons, making choices now that will resonate later. It means taking creative ownership not just of the pilot, but of everything that grows from it.

With ChatGPT, you're never writing in isolation. You're shaping a show, building a world, and guiding a story that extends far beyond page one. And that's not just useful—it's essential. Because in the current landscape, a pilot doesn't just need to impress. It needs to *prove* you can run the show.

And with the right questions, the right tools, and the right mindset—you absolutely can.

Writing the First Draft in Record Time

There's nothing like the energy of a first draft—the creative chaos, the rush of discovery, the excitement of seeing your world come alive on the page. But let's be honest: it can also be overwhelming. You're building a story, developing characters, trying to make every scene land, and keeping one eye on pacing, tone, structure, and dialogue. For many writers, the first draft becomes a slow crawl through self-doubt and endless rewrites. But it doesn't have to be that way. With the help of ChatGPT, you can write your first draft faster than ever—and better than you thought possible. It's like having a co-writer who never runs out of ideas, never gets tired, and is always ready to brainstorm, suggest, tweak, and push you forward.

Writing a pilot fast doesn't mean rushing blindly. It means focusing on progress over perfection. The goal of the first draft is to get the story down—not to make it pretty. You're sculpting the rough shape of your show, and rough is okay. In fact, rough is necessary. That's where ChatGPT shines. You can lean on it to fill in scenes, suggest dialogue, structure acts, and build emotional beats—all while you steer the ship. You stay in creative control, but you're never stuck staring at a blank page.

The best way to start fast is by creating a roadmap. Even a loose one. ChatGPT can help you outline your pilot in minutes. Try asking, "Give me a three-act breakdown for a character-driven mystery pilot" or "What are five turning points in a drama about a family falling apart?" Once you have that structure, even if it changes later, you've got guideposts. Now you're not writing into a void—you're writing toward something. This alone can shave days off your writing process.

Now take that outline and let ChatGPT help you expand it, one scene at a time. If you know you need a confrontation between two siblings in act one, ask, "Write a dramatic scene where two estranged siblings argue about their mother's will, but one of them is hiding something." You don't have to use the exact result, but it'll give you a strong starting point. Edit, tweak, personalize. Boom—one scene done. Now move to the next. The more you use ChatGPT as your creative jumpstart, the faster your script takes shape.

Dialogue slowing you down? Don't waste hours agonizing over the perfect line. Ask ChatGPT, "What's a tense but subtle way for this character to express jealousy?" or "How would this character threaten someone without sounding cliché?" You'll get a batch of lines to choose from, remix, or rewrite. You stay in control of the tone and intent, but now you're generating options at lightning speed.

Stuck on transitions? Let's say you've got two great scenes, but no idea how to connect them. Ask, "What's a brief, visual transition between a tense courtroom scene and a quiet domestic moment?" or "Give me a one-line cutaway that echoes the theme of justice." In seconds, you've got bridges between scenes that keep your momentum alive.

Pacing is another area where ChatGPT can supercharge your draft. If a section feels sluggish or uneven, drop it in and say, "Can you speed up the pacing of this scene without losing emotional impact?" Or if a moment feels rushed, say, "What beats could I add to slow this scene down and give it more weight?" This kind of immediate feedback is usually something you'd wait days or weeks to get from another reader—but now it's at your fingertips in real time.

Even writer's block isn't a threat when you've got a creative partner on demand. You can literally type, "I'm stuck. My protagonist needs to make a decision, but I'm not sure what's at stake," and ChatGPT will talk it through with you. It doesn't just offer plot points—it asks smart questions, surfaces alternatives, and helps you see your own ideas more clearly.

Let's not forget the value of variation. One of the fastest ways to improve a scene is to explore multiple versions quickly. Take a climactic confrontation and ask, "Give me three ways this argument could escalate—one tragic, one funny, one quiet but intense." Now you're not stuck polishing a single idea—you're choosing the strongest path from several great ones.

You can also use ChatGPT to generate subplots, layer theme, suggest callbacks, or reinforce tone—all in parallel with your writing. If you're working on a subplot about a romance gone wrong, just ask, "What's a subplot that mirrors this romance but ends in betrayal?" or "How can I echo this romantic tension in the main plot?" These additions deepen your script while keeping your focus sharp—and they happen in real time, without halting your writing flow.

The beauty of writing with ChatGPT is that it doesn't replace your creativity—it frees it. Instead of slogging through a clunky first draft, you're working at speed, riding a wave of momentum, discovering new angles, and finishing pages that might have taken days in a traditional process. You're drafting with velocity, shaping as you go, and staying emotionally connected to the story without getting stuck in perfection paralysis.

So if you've been putting off your pilot, waiting for the perfect inspiration or the perfect moment—don't. Just start. Open your outline. Type the first scene header. Ask ChatGPT for a nudge, a suggestion, a line of dialogue, a better transition, a stronger hook. And watch the pages fly by.

Writing a pilot in record time doesn't mean compromising quality. It means writing *bravely*, writing *efficiently*, and writing with the confidence that you've got a tool in your corner to help every step of the way.

This isn't just writing fast—it's writing smart. And the first draft? It's already waiting for you.

Getting Past Writer's Block with AI

Writer's block is the creative equivalent of quicksand. One minute you're cruising through your script, fully immersed in the world you're building, and the next you're stuck—staring at a blinking cursor, rewriting the same sentence over and over, doubting every choice you've made. It's frustrating, exhausting, and worst of all, isolating. But it doesn't have to be. Because with AI—specifically ChatGPT—you're never writing alone. You've got an always-available creative partner ready to brainstorm, reshape, redirect, or just talk you through the moment. And once you realize that, writer's block becomes a speed bump, not a dead end.

The key to beating writer's block isn't brute force—it's momentum. You don't need to write something perfect. You just need to write *something*. Anything that moves you forward, even if it changes later. That's where ChatGPT is invaluable. If you're stuck on a scene, you can literally say, "I don't know what happens next—can you give me three options that would escalate the tension?" Within seconds, you're looking at possibilities. They might not be the final version, but they'll spark new thoughts. And that spark is often all you need to get going again.

Sometimes the block isn't about the scene—it's about the character. You've written them into a corner, or their motivation suddenly feels off, or you're not sure how they'd react. That's when you turn to ChatGPT like a writer's room partner and say, "Here's what this character has gone through so far. What would feel like an honest, unexpected reaction in this moment?" You're not waiting for inspiration—you're co-developing it in real time. And once the character's voice returns, the writing tends to follow.

A great trick is to describe your block to ChatGPT exactly as it feels. Be honest. Say something like, "I'm writing a scene where my protagonist has to confess a lie, but I'm not sure how to make it emotional without sounding cliché." ChatGPT doesn't just throw you ideas—it helps reframe the problem. It might ask a question you hadn't considered or suggest a shift in tone or setting that unlocks everything. It's like having a script consultant in your pocket, one that doesn't get tired or judgy.

You can also use AI to test different narrative angles quickly. If you're struggling with how a scene should play out, say, "What if this scene ended with a betrayal instead of a reconciliation? What would that look like?" Or, "Can you write this scene as if it were from the antagonist's point of view?" Even if you don't use the suggestions directly, they'll shake your brain loose and get you thinking in fresh directions. Writer's block often thrives in repetition. ChatGPT is a pattern breaker.

Dialogue is another place where block tends to strike hard. You know the emotional beat, but the words won't come. That's a perfect time to hand the wheel over temporarily. Say, "Write a conversation between these two characters where one is trying to apologize, but the other doesn't believe them." You'll get a rough draft you can sculpt, rewrite, or even reject—but you're no longer staring at a blank page. You're editing, and editing is a lot easier than inventing from scratch.

You can also use ChatGPT to simplify. Sometimes writer's block comes from overcomplicating a scene. You're trying to make it too clever, too layered, too "perfect." Ask ChatGPT, "What's the simplest version of this scene that still hits the emotional note?" or "What would happen if I just let this moment breathe without over-explaining it?" The AI can help strip away the noise and show you the clean, emotional core of what you're trying to say.

Let's not forget the mental side of writer's block—the voice that says, "You're wasting time," or "This idea isn't good enough," or "You're not doing it right." That voice thrives in isolation. Using ChatGPT breaks that silence. You're not just fighting your own doubts—you're collaborating. Even just typing, "I feel stuck on this story beat and don't know if it works," can lead to reassurance, analysis, and new solutions. That dialogue—yes, with a machine—can be surprisingly freeing.

Sometimes what you really need is to zoom out. You've been in the weeds of one scene for hours, and it's clouding your view. Use ChatGPT to look at the bigger picture. Ask, "What's the point of this scene in the overall episode arc?" or "What emotional beat should this scene be leading toward?" When you refocus on the *why*, the *how* gets a lot easier.

You can even play writing games with the AI to shake things loose. Say, "Give me a random setting, a secret, and a conflict," and see what comes up. Or "Write this moment as a silent scene—no dialogue." Or "How would this scene play out if it were in a romantic comedy instead of a thriller?" These creative detours can reveal new tones, twists, and textures that refresh your process.

And if you're completely blocked—totally blank, no idea where to go next—there's nothing wrong with jumping ahead. Ask ChatGPT to help you write a future scene. The climax. A quiet character moment in episode two. An alternate version of the cold open. Writing out of order is not failure—it's strategy. Once you get back in flow, you can circle around and fill in the gaps.

At the end of the day, writer's block is about pressure: the pressure to be brilliant, original, efficient, on-theme, and moving the plot forward—all at once. It's a lot. But ChatGPT gives you the space to be messy, experimental, and curious. It helps you get *something* on the page—because something is always better than nothing.

So next time you hit that wall, don't power through it alone. Ask a question. Get a second opinion. Try a new angle. Let AI be your sounding board, your co-pilot, your idea factory.

You'll be surprised how quickly the block dissolves when you stop writing *alone*.

Making the Rewrite Phase Less Painful

Let's be real: rewriting can feel like a cruel joke. You've just spent hours—days, maybe weeks—writing your pilot, and now, instead of celebrating, you're being told to tear it apart. Cut scenes you love. Kill dialogue you thought was perfect. Restructure entire acts. It's exhausting, emotional, and sometimes demoralizing. But here's the secret no one tells you when you're starting out: rewriting is *where the real writing happens*. The first draft is raw material. The rewrite is where your pilot becomes *watchable*. It's where everything sharpens—your characters deepen, your pacing tightens, your story finally starts to sing. And with ChatGPT in your corner, the rewrite doesn't have to feel like a slow, solo death march. It can be strategic, supportive, even exciting.

The first shift is mental. Stop thinking of the rewrite as a punishment. It's not about fixing what's broken—it's about *refining what works*. You've already done the hardest part: you finished the draft. Now you've got something to sculpt. And ChatGPT gives you a way to approach it analytically rather than emotionally. Instead of feeling like you're gutting your favorite scenes, you're testing, iterating, improving. That alone makes the process easier to handle.

Start by getting a bird's eye view. Paste your pilot summary or outline into ChatGPT and ask, "What elements of this story feel the weakest or most underdeveloped?" or "Where does the tension drop in this pilot?" The AI can help you see structural or tonal issues you might not be able to spot yourself because you're too close to the material. Once those areas are identified, you're not guessing—you're *targeting* your rewrite.

One of the hardest parts of rewriting is knowing what to cut. Every line feels like it matters. But when you ask ChatGPT, "Which parts of this scene are slowing down the pacing?" or "Is this conversation revealing anything new, or just repeating information?" you start to identify redundancies and dead air. The AI gives you permission to trim—and often suggests cleaner, sharper ways to say what you're trying to say. That can turn a painful cut into a clear improvement.

Dialogue rewrites? Way less painful with help. If a scene feels flat, you can say, "Rewrite this exchange so there's more emotional tension," or "Can you make this line sound more like a veiled threat instead of a cliché?" You'll get variations instantly. Not to replace your voice, but to give you new angles, new energy, and better rhythm. And when you're working through thirty or forty scenes, that time saved is no small thing.

Let's talk about restructuring—probably the most dreaded part of any rewrite. Maybe a big twist is happening too late. Maybe your cold open isn't doing its job. Instead of spending hours moving index cards around, ask ChatGPT, "How would this pilot change if I moved this reveal to the beginning?" or "What would a new structure look like if I started with the climax and worked backwards?" You're not starting from scratch—you're running simulations, fast. And you can compare multiple approaches in minutes, not days.

Rewriting also means finding moments to go *deeper*. That doesn't have to be painful—it can actually be the most fun part. Ask ChatGPT, "How can I strengthen the emotional impact of this scene?" or "What's a visual callback I could add here to echo an earlier moment?" These aren't just edits—they're upgrades. You're building connections, adding subtext, and giving your story more resonance.

Don't forget character development. During the rewrite, you might realize one character feels flat or inconsistent. Ask ChatGPT to do a character audit. Try, "Based on these scenes, does this character's arc feel clear?" or "What's a subtle way to show this character's internal conflict without dialogue?" You'll get insight that helps unify the character from scene to scene. Suddenly that confusing emotional turn makes sense—and your rewrite feels like discovery, not damage control.

Tone is another thing that's easy to lose track of during a rewrite. You add a joke here, cut a dramatic beat there, and before you know it, your gritty thriller feels like a quirky dramedy. Ask ChatGPT, "Does this scene still match the tone of the show I'm building?" or "How can I bring this scene's tone back in line with the rest of the script?" These little adjustments help you keep the pilot emotionally cohesive.

Let's not ignore the emotional toll. Rewriting can mess with your confidence. That's where ChatGPT can double as your pep talk machine. When you're feeling stuck, ask, "Remind me why this story is worth telling," or "What's compelling about my protagonist that makes this show worth watching?" It might sound silly, but sometimes what we need is a reminder that the heart of the story is still beating strong—even if the current draft is a little bruised.

And when the rewrite feels never-ending, ChatGPT can help you set manageable goals. Say, "Help me break this rewrite into five focused passes," and it might suggest a structure like pass one for pacing, pass two for character, pass three for dialogue, pass four for theme, and pass five for polish. Now your rewrite is a roadmap, not a foggy wilderness.

You don't have to do it all at once. And you don't have to do it alone. ChatGPT gives you support at every level—from the smallest line tweak to the biggest plot restructure. It takes the pressure off your shoulders and lets you stay in motion, stay creative, and actually enjoy the process of watching your pilot evolve.

Because at the end of the day, rewriting isn't about fixing mistakes. It's about unlocking the better version of the story that's already *in there*—waiting to be uncovered.

And with AI as your sidekick, finding that version just got a whole lot easier.

Creating Scene Breakdowns with ChatGPT

Writing a pilot is one thing—*organizing* it is another. A great idea can get lost in translation without clear structure, especially when scenes start stacking up and momentum becomes hard to manage. That's where scene breakdowns come in. A scene breakdown is essentially your story's skeletal system. It lets you map out the sequence of events, monitor pacing, track character arcs, and see how every piece contributes to the bigger picture. But building one can be a grind—unless you're working with ChatGPT. With AI in your corner, you can not only generate scene breakdowns faster but also shape them in a way that brings out the most emotional and narrative power from every beat.

Let's start simple: what is a scene breakdown, really? It's a list of scenes—sometimes as bullet points, sometimes as paragraphs—where each entry describes what happens, who's involved, what changes emotionally or plot-wise, and what the purpose of the scene is. Think of it as a step between the outline and the script. You're figuring out the rhythm of the episode before committing to full pages of dialogue and description. It's also the perfect place to identify which scenes are truly essential—and which ones are just filler.

With ChatGPT, you can build a full scene breakdown with just your logline, a character list, and a rough idea of your story's beginning, middle, and end. Start by feeding in a basic pitch: "My story is about a young nurse who discovers a conspiracy at the hospital where she works." Then ask, "Can you create a 10-scene breakdown for the pilot episode?" In seconds, you'll have a list of story beats with rising tension, emotional development, and pacing that's built for episodic TV.

But don't stop there. Once you have your rough breakdown, use ChatGPT to workshop each individual scene. Say, "Let's look at Scene 3. I want this to be where the protagonist first suspects something is off—can you give me options for what she might see or hear that raises her suspicions?" You're now using AI as a story lab, testing versions of scenes without burning time writing and rewriting them from scratch.

Need to track emotional arcs? Ask, "In this scene, what's the emotional shift for the protagonist?" or "How does this scene push the character further from or closer to their goal?" Scene breakdowns aren't just about what *happens*—they're about *why it matters*. ChatGPT can help you build emotional continuity by making sure each scene leaves the characters changed in some way.

A huge bonus of doing your scene breakdown with ChatGPT is the ability to troubleshoot pacing *before* you hit script stage. If you're worried your pilot gets bogged down in exposition early on, ask, "Which of these scenes are heavy on information, and how can I break that up with conflict or action?" Or, "Where should I place a tension spike to keep the momentum up?" You'll get suggestions that can transform dry stretches into dynamic storytelling.

You can also use ChatGPT to balance your character focus. Ask, "Does this scene breakdown give enough screen time to the supporting cast?" or "Where can I give the antagonist a stronger presence in act one?" The AI can suggest insert scenes, small moments, or entire side beats that help you round out the ensemble. This is critical in a pilot, where you're setting up the emotional architecture for the series.

If you're working with an ensemble or multi-plot format, ChatGPT is especially useful for mapping parallel storylines. Ask, "Can you interweave the protagonist's arc with a subplot involving her brother who's a police officer?" or "How can I alternate scenes to keep both threads advancing without losing clarity?" Suddenly you're not just breaking scenes—you're braiding narratives.

And let's not forget theme. Scene breakdowns are a great place to plant and grow your theme across the episode. Ask, "How can each scene reflect the theme of trust and betrayal in subtle ways?" or "Which scene should deliver the emotional thesis of the episode, and how?" These questions elevate your structure from functional to *meaningful.*

When it's time to rewrite, your scene breakdown becomes your map. If something's not working, it's easier to change it here than on the page. Say, "Scene 6 feels repetitive—what else could happen in this moment that still advances the protagonist's arc?" ChatGPT can pitch alternatives that stay true to your tone and plot. You're not locked in—you're refining as you go.

You can also use your breakdown to build in visual storytelling. Ask, "What's a visual way to express isolation in Scene 2?" or "How can I open Scene 5 with an image that foreshadows the climax?" With ChatGPT helping brainstorm cinematic touches, your scenes stop being just plot delivery systems and start becoming moments that *feel* like television.

Finally, once your breakdown is solid, you can use it to draft faster. Copy a scene summary and say, "Turn this breakdown into a three-page script scene," and ChatGPT will give you a first pass—dialogue, action, and all. You can take it from there, rewriting, fine-tuning, or riffing off the structure. But now you're never starting from zero.

So if you've been stuck trying to figure out how to get from story idea to finished pilot, don't overlook scene breakdowns—and don't do them alone. With ChatGPT, you can move quickly, stay organized, and explore your story from multiple angles before you write a single slug line.

It's not just about planning. It's about unlocking creative clarity, one scene at a time.

Using ChatGPT to Explore What-If Story Paths

One of the most exciting (and sometimes overwhelming) parts of writing a TV pilot is realizing just how many directions your story could go. A single character choice can change the tone of an entire episode. A different scene order might make a subplot hit harder. A story twist could reframe your protagonist in ways you hadn't expected. These forks in the road are where creativity really kicks in—but they can also be paralysing when you're working alone. That's where ChatGPT becomes your secret storytelling engine. With a few keystrokes, you can explore "what-if" scenarios in your pilot without committing to long rewrites. It's like having an infinite brainstorming partner who can map out alternate realities for your story—quickly, clearly, and creatively.

"What-if" questions are how writers find the most unexpected and powerful versions of their story. What if your protagonist made the *wrong* choice in that critical scene? What if the antagonist turned out to be the hero's long-lost sibling? What if the first ten minutes of your pilot happened in reverse? Asking these questions opens the door to new stakes, new emotional beats, and new themes. The challenge is that exploring these ideas in depth usually takes time. With ChatGPT, it takes seconds. You can pose a question like, "What if my main character chooses to lie instead of telling the truth in Scene 3—how would that change the rest of the episode?" and instantly get a branching path laid out in front of you.

This process is great for character development. Let's say your protagonist is a young cop who's just discovered a piece of evidence that implicates their partner. You've written them as conflicted, ultimately choosing loyalty over justice. But what if they chose the opposite? You can ask ChatGPT, "How would the story shift if my protagonist turned in their partner in episode one?" Now you've got a version of your story that explores consequences, changes relationship dynamics, and maybe even launches a whole different kind of show. And even if you don't go with that path, exploring it sharpens your understanding of the version you *do* want to tell.

"What-if" exploration is also perfect for tone experiments. If you're not sure what kind of show you're writing, you can play with genre to discover new potential. Ask ChatGPT, "What if this story about a grief counsellor was written as a dark comedy instead of a drama?" or "How would the opening scene of this thriller work if I rewrote it with the tone of a romantic dramedy?" These shifts can lead to surprisingly original hybrids—or help you clarify the emotional DNA of the version you love most.

You can use this same technique to explore structure. Maybe your pilot is told in a linear format—but what if you shook that up? Ask, "What if I started this episode with the climactic moment, then worked backwards to reveal how we got there?" or "What if each scene followed a different character's point of view?" ChatGPT will outline how that approach would impact pacing, character arcs, and the overall hook of your story. This kind of experimentation is how bold, unconventional pilots are born.

Sometimes the best use of "what-if" storytelling is to fix a problem. Maybe the midpoint of your episode is sagging. You're not sure what's supposed to happen there. Ask ChatGPT, "What if something unexpected or shocking happened in this scene—what are five possibilities that still connect to my theme of betrayal?" This can turn a dead patch in your script into a major turning point. You're not just patching a hole—you're upgrading the whole emotional engine.

Don't be afraid to explore alternate character relationships, either. A simple change like, "What if these two characters used to date?" or "What if this mentor is actually working against the protagonist?" can add emotional complexity, narrative tension, and long-term story fuel. ChatGPT can quickly walk you through how those dynamics would play out across the pilot—and into future episodes.

Another brilliant way to use ChatGPT is for theme testing. You might be writing about justice, but what if the real theme is redemption? Or identity? Ask, "What if I reframed this story as being about forgiveness instead of revenge—how would that affect the character arcs?" You'll get not just plot changes, but emotional shifts that make your story more resonant and focused. These "what-if" questions aren't just creative—they're clarifying.

When you find a version of a scene or story path you love, you can then ask ChatGPT to generate the dialogue or action for that version. It's like building out a new draft without starting from scratch. You've already made the big decision—you're just letting the tool help you sketch it in quickly. For example, "Give me a rewrite of Scene 6 where the protagonist walks away from the deal instead of taking it" can yield an entirely new emotional tone and plot trajectory—one you might never have tried on your own.

You can even ask ChatGPT to give you multiple variations side by side. Say, "Give me three versions of the final scene—one where the protagonist wins, one where they lose, and one where they walk away from the conflict entirely." Then you can compare them for tone, stakes, and setup for the next episode. It's like seeing alternate timelines, all laid out for you to choose from.

What's most liberating about exploring "what-if" story paths with AI is that it removes the fear of wasting time. You're not committing to a rewrite—you're sampling possibilities. You can try the wild version. The subtle version. The emotional version. The risky version. And in doing so, you often stumble on the *right* version—the one that surprises you and excites you and suddenly makes the whole episode work.

So the next time you feel stuck in your pilot, or something feels flat or predictable, ask yourself: "What if...?" And then ask ChatGPT to help you answer it. You're not just writing a story—you're exploring the *multiverse* of your story. And that's where some of your best ideas are hiding—just one question away.

Working Backwards from the Series Finale

One of the most powerful tools you can use when writing a pilot is something most writers save for last—or never do at all. That tool is working backwards from the series finale. It sounds counterintuitive at first. Why start with the end when you haven't even nailed the beginning? But when you know where your story is ultimately going, every choice you make in the pilot becomes sharper, more intentional, and more emotionally charged. You stop writing guesswork and start building toward something. And when you use ChatGPT to help chart this journey from end to beginning, you give yourself a blueprint that makes your entire series feel designed, not improvised.

Thinking about your series finale doesn't mean locking yourself into every detail. You're not writing the last episode now—you're identifying the emotional and thematic destination. What does your protagonist have to face? What will they become? What unresolved conflict will finally explode or resolve? How does the world you've created change—or not—by the end? You can ask ChatGPT, "What's a powerful emotional ending for a story about a woman who's been hiding her identity for years?" or "What's a final episode idea that brings justice full circle in a legal drama?" These prompts help you think about the kind of *impact* you want your series to leave behind.

Once you know your endgame, the pilot becomes about planting seeds. Think about the emotional arc. If your finale shows the protagonist accepting their flaws, then your pilot should show them resisting or hiding from those same flaws. If the finale reveals a major betrayal, then the pilot can introduce the relationship that will eventually fracture. With ChatGPT, you can reverse-engineer this arc. Say, "If the main character sacrifices their ambition for love in the finale, what should their mindset be in the pilot?" The AI will give you a clear contrast—and that contrast is your arc.

Plot-wise, working backwards keeps you from wandering. You're no longer making things up as you go. You're creating setups for future payoffs. That mysterious side character in episode one? Maybe they're the key to the entire ending. That emotional wound the protagonist hides? It's going to break open later. Ask ChatGPT, "What story elements can I introduce in the pilot that will pay off in the series finale?" It might suggest props, phrases, relationships, or unresolved questions that create continuity and tension across the series.

You can also use this approach to shape subplots. Let's say your finale features the main character finally reconciling with a sibling they've been estranged from for years. Now the pilot can drop hints of that rift. A silent phone call. A photo turned face down. A line of dialogue that goes unanswered. ChatGPT can help brainstorm those subtle clues with a prompt like, "What are small visual or emotional beats that foreshadow a long-buried family conflict?"

Tone and theme also benefit from a backwards-first approach. If your finale ends on hope after seasons of despair, then the pilot should lean into the bleakness—so the transformation feels earned. If your story ends in moral ambiguity, then the pilot might start with a clear-cut sense of right and wrong. Ask ChatGPT, "What is a thematic arc that begins with justice and ends with compromise?" or "How can the tone evolve from whimsical to tragic across a season arc?" and you'll get ideas that guide your tone shifts with purpose.

One underrated benefit of this method is it helps you avoid writing yourself into a corner. Many series start strong but stumble because they don't know how to end. But when you've already envisioned the destination—even loosely—you can build toward it instead of writing around it. You'll start to see which characters have long-term potential, which mysteries can sustain multiple episodes, and which plotlines will need room to grow. ChatGPT can act as your series planner here. Try, "Outline a five-season journey that ends with the protagonist's death," or "Give me a slow-burn mystery that starts in the pilot and resolves in the finale."

Working backwards also lets you shape your world more efficiently. If you know a certain location will become significant later, you can introduce it in the pilot as an everyday space—then watch it change meaning as the series evolves. A small-town diner in episode one might seem cozy and irrelevant—until it becomes the site of a major revelation in the final season. ChatGPT can help brainstorm symbolic or practical locations that evolve with your story.

When it comes to relationships, this technique is gold. If two characters end the series as bitter enemies, show them as allies in the pilot. If a couple finally comes together in the finale, plant the first spark—or the first awkward silence—right away. You can ask ChatGPT, "What's an early interaction between two characters that sets up a future romantic arc?" or "What's a misdirect I can use to hide that these two will eventually fall out?"

Working backwards doesn't limit your creativity—it *frees* it. You stop second-guessing your story's direction and start building with confidence. You start seeing the pilot not as an isolated episode, but as the opening move in a carefully orchestrated strategy. And viewers feel that. They sense when a show knows where it's going. It makes your storytelling feel tighter, smarter, and more satisfying.

So before you dive back into rewriting your pilot, pause and imagine the end. Even if it changes later, it gives you something to aim for. Then, step by step, scene by scene, work your way back to page one. With ChatGPT guiding the way, you can test versions, run character arcs, and develop a story that feels complete from beginning to end—even if the audience only sees episode one for now.

Because a truly great pilot doesn't just hook us—it *whispers* where this story is headed. And that's the kind of storytelling people stick with. Not because they know the ending—but because they can *feel* it coming.

Building Suspense and Mystery into the Pilot

If you want your pilot to grip viewers and not let go, suspense and mystery are your most valuable tools. They're the secret ingredients that keep people watching, wondering, speculating, and clicking "Next Episode" without hesitation. Suspense isn't just for thrillers and mysteries—it's a universal storytelling engine. Every genre benefits from a question the audience *has* to see answered. Whether it's "Who killed her?" or "What's she hiding?" or "Why is this town so weird?", the key to a magnetic pilot is making the viewer lean forward from scene one. And with ChatGPT at your side, you can build, test, and fine-tune those narrative hooks with surprising ease, crafting a story that's not just interesting—it's irresistible.

Suspense starts with information control. Who knows what, when? You don't want to dump everything on the audience at once. You want to give them *just enough* to stay curious. In your pilot, the most compelling tool you have is *withholding*. Not confusing the viewer—just teasing them. Show the consequences before the cause. Start with a character acting strangely, then slowly reveal what's driving that behavior. Or show a mysterious event with no explanation, then drop small clues throughout the episode. You can ask ChatGPT, "What's a strong visual hook for a pilot that raises immediate questions?" and it will pitch you scenes that open with intrigue instead of exposition.

Mystery is most effective when it feels personal. It's not just about an external puzzle; it's about emotional stakes. What makes the audience *care* about the mystery? A missing person is more gripping when it's someone the protagonist deeply loves—or deeply fears. A secret is more intense when it could destroy a relationship we've started to root for. Use ChatGPT to build those stakes early on: "What's a character secret that would complicate a new romance?" or "What's a mystery that ties directly into the protagonist's deepest fear?" The goal is to make the unknown feel urgent.

One of the most underused tricks in building suspense is *the question with no immediate answer*. You introduce a visual or moment that doesn't make sense—yet. A character burying something in the woods. A child who refuses to speak when asked about a specific person. A side character acting strangely when a certain name is mentioned. These moments don't pay off right away—they just sit there, creating tension. Viewers don't need the answer right away—they just need to know there *is* one. Ask ChatGPT, "Give me a list of five mysterious actions a character could take in the pilot that suggest a hidden agenda," and you'll get instant fuel for suspense.

The pacing of your reveals matters too. Suspense isn't a constant scream—it's a rhythm. A good pilot teases, builds, distracts, then reveals *something*—but not everything. Think of it like opening a door just enough to glimpse something inside, but not enough to step through yet. ChatGPT can help you map this rhythm. Say, "Can you help structure the mystery reveals in my pilot so they escalate across three acts?" Now you're layering tension in a way that's deliberate and satisfying.

One great way to keep suspense tight is to build scenes around *desire and danger*. What does the protagonist want—and what's in the way? What are they afraid of being exposed? A scene where a character lies to cover up a mistake is more suspenseful than one where they explain their backstory. A scene where two characters talk around a secret is more compelling than one where they explain it outright. Ask ChatGPT, "What's a suspenseful version of this scene where the protagonist is hiding something from their best friend?" and you'll get dialogue and staging that crackles with tension.

Tone plays a huge part too. Even if your story isn't a thriller, you can borrow thriller techniques to keep your audience engaged. A slow pan in a quiet room. A sudden silence in the middle of a conversation. An object that doesn't belong.

These visual cues create mood and unease. Ask ChatGPT, "What's a way to build an unsettling atmosphere in this scene without using dialogue?" and you'll get ideas that rely on setting, sound, and subtext to build suspense visually.

Suspense also thrives in contradictions. A character saying they're fine—but locking the door behind them. A town that seems peaceful—but everyone avoids talking about one house. These subtle inconsistencies create unease. The viewer starts to realize things aren't what they seem. You can use ChatGPT to develop those cracks in the surface: "What are ways to make this setting seem normal on the surface but disturbing underneath?" or "What contradictions could this character embody that hint at a hidden life?"

And then there are the reveals. You can't keep piling mystery without giving the audience something. The trick is to reveal *enough* to satisfy them while raising new questions. A reveal that answers one mystery but opens another is the engine of bingeable storytelling. Use ChatGPT to finesse this balance: "How can I resolve this scene's tension while setting up a bigger twist?" or "What's a reveal that shifts the viewer's perspective on what they've already seen?" These moves turn your pilot into a puzzle that viewers love putting together.

If your show is meant to run on suspense and mystery long-term, use your pilot to establish the *rules*. How much does the audience know compared to the characters? Are we ahead, behind, or right beside them in knowledge? ChatGPT can help you test those choices. Try, "How does this story change if the audience knows the twist before the protagonist?" or "What's the impact of withholding this reveal until the final scene of the pilot?" Exploring these variations can lead to breakthroughs in tone and structure.

Most importantly, make sure the suspense *matters*. It's not just about tricks—it's about trust. The audience will stick with you if they feel you're building toward something meaningful. Every withheld fact, every raised question, every eerie moment—they're all promises. Your job in the pilot is to make those promises compelling enough that the viewer *has* to see where it all leads.

And with ChatGPT helping you test, build, and evolve your mystery elements, you don't have to figure it all out at once. You can brainstorm five versions of a twist, run a dozen alternate cold opens, explore different secrets for each character—all before you even write the final draft.

Because mystery isn't just about what's hidden. It's about what's *waiting to be discovered*. And if your pilot is built on that kind of invitation, your audience won't just watch it. They'll *follow it.*

Setting the Rules of the World in the First Episode

Every TV series lives in its own unique world—whether it's a heightened reality, a grounded drama, a fantastical universe, or something strange and in between. The world doesn't just set the backdrop for your story; it determines what's possible, what's normal, what's dangerous, and what the characters can get away with. And if your audience doesn't understand the rules of the world by the end of the first episode, they're going to feel lost or confused—or worse, they'll stop watching. That's why one of your biggest responsibilities in writing a pilot is to quietly, confidently teach the audience how your world works. And with ChatGPT, you can pressure-test those rules, build them out faster, and make sure they're woven into your pilot without slowing down the story.

So, what do we mean by "the rules of the world"? It's not just geography or lore. It's *how life operates here*. What kind of authority is in charge? What are the unspoken cultural norms? Is there magic? Is technology more advanced or less? Is morality rigid or fluid? Is violence normal? Is time linear? These questions might sound big and abstract, but they need to be answered on the page, even if only subtly. And every answer becomes a rule.

The best pilots don't dump these rules on the audience. They demonstrate them. You show the world in action. For example, if your story takes place in a future where social credit scores determine your status, don't start with an explanation—start with a character being publicly humiliated or denied entry somewhere because their score dropped. Ask ChatGPT, "What's a powerful visual way to show that status is controlled by a social score system?" and you'll get dramatic beats that convey the rule *through story*.

A great exercise is to list the top five rules your world operates by, then ask: "How can I show each of these within the first ten pages?" Not tell—*show*. You want the audience to understand what's allowed, what's taboo, what's dangerous, and what's expected. If you're writing a supernatural story, the audience needs to know what the creatures can and can't do. If you're writing a political drama, they need to know what power looks like—and who actually holds it. ChatGPT can help here with prompts like, "How do I organically introduce the fact that ghosts can't enter churches in this story?" or "What's a compelling scene where a low-level staffer realizes who really controls the city?"

It's also important to show how *your protagonist* fits into this world—or doesn't. Are they comfortable in it? Do they obey the rules or break them? Are they aware of the world's true nature, or are they discovering it along with us? Ask ChatGPT, "What's a character-defining moment that reveals my protagonist's relationship to the world's rules?" A character who flouts the law, for example, is signaling to the audience that rebellion is possible. A character who's terrified to speak up shows us this is a place where silence is survival.

One of the best ways to establish rules is through contrast. Introduce a character who *doesn't* follow the norm—and then show the consequences. This both highlights the rule and makes the world feel alive. If people in your world never walk outside without masks, introduce someone who does—and show how others react. Ask ChatGPT, "How can I use a newcomer character to highlight the rules of this world?" These "outsider" characters give the audience someone to identify with and learn through.

Language and behavior are also great ways to signal the world's structure. Characters in a formal dystopia might speak in clipped, official terms. In a lawless society, they might talk in code or use harsh slang. Ask ChatGPT, "What kind of vocabulary would characters use in a society where emotion is outlawed?" and you'll get a lexicon that reinforces the world on a subtle but powerful level.

Tone also plays a huge role in establishing your world. If your story is absurd, grim, ironic, or surreal, the tone you choose teaches the audience what kind of logic they're expected to accept. A satirical pilot might open with exaggerated behavior that sets the rules of comedy. A noir thriller might begin with moody silence and unease. Ask ChatGPT, "What kind of opening scene would signal that this world is both dangerous and surreal?" and you'll get ideas that carry tone, setting, and rules in one go.

Don't forget to hint at the *bigger world* too. The pilot doesn't need to show everything—but it should suggest depth. Let's say your character lives in a small town where everyone seems normal. You might drop one quick line where someone refers to "what happened upstate last year"—and suddenly the audience knows there's a wider, possibly darker history. ChatGPT can help craft those offhand references that feel natural but loaded. Try, "Give me five lines of dialogue that suggest a history of government collapse without explaining it outright."

And when your world has supernatural or sci-fi elements, clarity is everything. Ask ChatGPT, "What are the limitations of the magic system in this story, and how can I demonstrate them through conflict?" or "What's a situation where futuristic tech creates a moral dilemma that highlights the show's central theme?" These moments don't just explain the rules—they make them matter to the characters and the audience.

Above all, your rules should *serve the story*. They're not decoration. They're the boundaries your characters operate within, the pressures they live under, and the limits they'll try to break. When the audience understands those boundaries, they'll feel the stakes. They'll understand what's risky. They'll get what's at stake. And they'll want to see what happens when someone challenges the system.

With ChatGPT helping you explore, clarify, and implement those rules, you'll be able to construct a pilot that feels grounded, confident, and immersive. Whether your world is strange, dangerous, hilarious, or subtle, you'll be teaching the audience how to live in it without them even realizing they're learning.

And by the end of episode one, they won't just be watching the story—they'll be living in your world, and they won't want to leave.

Introducing Lore without Losing the Audience

Lore is the rich soil that your TV series grows from—it's the history, mythology, politics, culture, and secrets that give your world texture and depth. Whether your show is set in a dystopian future, a small town with a hidden past, or a magical realm with ancient rules, the lore helps the world feel real and lived-in. But lore is a double-edged sword. Go too heavy, and your audience gets overwhelmed or bored. Go too light, and they feel unmoored, like they're watching something thin and undercooked. The trick is to introduce just enough lore to intrigue, anchor, and guide—without turning your pilot into a history lecture. And with ChatGPT, you can shape and deliver that lore in subtle, powerful ways that keep the audience hooked instead of lost.

The biggest mistake writers make when introducing lore is front-loading it. Starting with a monologue, a block of text, or a clunky scene where characters explain the world to each other feels artificial and slows the story down. Instead of asking, "How do I explain this lore?" ask, "How can the audience *feel* this lore without needing to understand every detail right away?" ChatGPT can help you brainstorm these more organic delivery methods. For example, you could say, "What's a subtle way to introduce the idea of a fallen empire without a history lesson?" and it might suggest a crumbling statue, a classroom scene where a teacher skips over the topic, or a forbidden book glimpsed in passing.

You want your audience to feel like they're stepping into a fully functioning world that existed before the pilot started—and will keep existing after the episode ends. To do that, show characters interacting with the world's rules, not explaining them. Let someone bribe a border guard with a rare relic from the old war, or struggle to pray in a language they barely remember from childhood. These moments communicate *so much* without needing exposition. You can use ChatGPT to generate these tiny world-building beats: "Give me a list of actions that reveal a culture's religious oppression without saying it directly."

One effective technique is to use lore as seasoning, not the main course. Sprinkle it throughout scenes as if the characters already know it. Let them reference places, people, or events in passing—things they'd never explain because they live in that world. It makes the lore feel real. Think of it like overhearing a conversation you weren't invited to—your curiosity does the rest. Try prompting ChatGPT with, "Write dialogue where two characters casually reference an old war, but don't explain it," and you'll start to see how tone and rhythm can carry a sense of depth.

A great strategy is to anchor new lore in *emotional context*. People remember feelings more than facts. If a character gets visibly shaken at the mention of a certain name, the audience feels the weight of that history even if they don't know the details. A symbol carved into a wall. A moment of fear or reverence at the sight of a uniform. Ask ChatGPT, "What's a visual moment that suggests a dark historical event without dialogue?" These images create emotional anchors that make the lore land without info-dumping.

Another way to ease in lore is through *point of view*. If your protagonist is new to this world—or if they're discovering a hidden layer of it—that gives you a natural reason to let the audience learn with them. But don't turn it into a school lesson. Let the discoveries come with conflict, curiosity, or danger. ChatGPT can help you shape that introduction: "How can my protagonist uncover forbidden lore through a mistake or accident?" Now the information comes with stakes and tension.

Mystery is your friend. Don't give away everything. Instead of explaining the full backstory of a war, mention a nickname that suggests brutality. Instead of explaining the council's authority, show someone disobeying an order—and the swift punishment that follows. Ask ChatGPT, "What's a mysterious phrase or object that hints at larger lore?" These hints become narrative hooks, drawing the viewer deeper into the world.

Characters are also your delivery system. Let their opinions about the world reveal the layers. One character might revere a fallen hero, while another spits on the ground at the mention of their name. This contrast not only teaches the audience about the world—it adds depth to your characters. Try asking ChatGPT, "Give me two opposing character views on a historic event from this world," and you'll start to see how conflict itself can carry exposition.

Flashbacks, dreams, rituals, objects, and music can all carry lore too—but use them sparingly. One symbol on a ring might say more about legacy and power than a five-minute scene in a royal court. Ask ChatGPT, "How can I use a single object to represent generations of conflict in this world?" and you'll find ways to tell stories with fewer words and more impact.

If you're worried about clarity, use ChatGPT as your story compass. Drop in a scene and say, "Will a viewer understand what they need to know here, or is this too vague?" Or, "What's missing in this scene to help the audience follow the lore without confusion?" The AI will walk through it with you like a curious but critical first-time viewer—exactly the perspective you need.

One of the most powerful things you can do is trust your audience. Viewers don't need to know everything in the first episode. They just need to *feel* that everything has meaning. The best shows let you feel the weight of history before you even know what that history is. With ChatGPT helping you balance intrigue, clarity, and emotion, you can introduce your lore in a way that's elegant and effective—inviting the audience to lean in, not lean back.

Because great lore doesn't beg for attention. It waits patiently, woven into the world, daring the audience to look closer. And when it's introduced right, that curiosity becomes the engine that keeps your entire series running.

Exploring Flashbacks and Time Shifts in the Pilot

When used well, flashbacks and time shifts can turn a good pilot into a layered, emotionally rich, and narratively compelling first episode. They're not just stylistic choices—they're storytelling tools that help you deepen character, build mystery, and reveal vital backstory without info-dumping. But when used clumsily, they can confuse the audience, disrupt pacing, or break emotional momentum. That's why exploring how and when to use time shifts is crucial in the early stages of your pilot. And with ChatGPT, you can test different structures, experiment with emotional reveals, and construct time jumps that feel seamless and intentional—all without getting stuck in the weeds.

Let's start with what flashbacks and time shifts actually do for your story. At their core, they're a way of collapsing time—of showing how the past still shapes the present. They let the audience see a character's trauma instead of hearing about it. They let you plant a clue from long ago that explains something happening now. And they allow you to contrast who someone *was* with who they are now, which adds emotional and thematic weight to everything they do. The key is not to use them just because they're cool—but because they add meaning to the now.

You can use ChatGPT to help decide if a flashback is truly necessary. Drop in your scene and ask, "Would this character beat be more powerful if we saw the moment that caused it?" or "Is there a past event I could dramatize here instead of having a character explain it?" Sometimes the answer is yes, and the flashback becomes your best scene. Other times, the suggestion is to let the present hold the emotion. Either way, you're using AI to help make the storytelling more purposeful.

The placement of flashbacks in your pilot matters a lot. Early on, they work best when tied directly to a present-moment trigger—a sound, a question, a location, a photograph, a silence. You don't want to break the flow just to show something interesting. You want to create a rhythm where the audience understands that we're leaving the present because something important is being emotionally or narratively unlocked. Ask ChatGPT, "What's a natural trigger in this scene that could spark a flashback?" and you'll start connecting memory to emotion in a grounded way.

There's also the question of *how* you present your time shifts. Are they quick visual flashes? Full scenes with their own structure? Stylized recreations? ChatGPT can help you explore format options: "Write a stylized flashback where everything is silent except for the sound of breathing," or "Give me a minimalist memory scene where the characters never make eye contact." Suddenly you're not just using flashbacks—you're using them *artistically*.

You might also experiment with time shifts that aren't flashbacks in the traditional sense. Nonlinear storytelling can be a powerful tool if handled clearly. Think of pilots like *Lost* or *The Witcher* that jump timelines to slowly reveal connections. Or *Breaking Bad* opening with a flash-forward, then rewinding to show how we got there. These kinds of time shifts give the viewer narrative puzzles to solve. With ChatGPT, you can test these structures before committing. Ask, "What if my pilot started with the ending, then circled back to the beginning—how would that change the pacing?" or "Outline a nonlinear structure that reveals my protagonist's secret over three scenes from different decades."

Flashbacks can also be character studies. You might use them not to explain plot but to highlight emotional patterns. A character makes a bad decision in the present, and you flash back to a childhood moment where they learned that behavior. This kind of echo deepens empathy and shows how the past keeps repeating. Try asking ChatGPT, "What's a flashback that mirrors my protagonist's current self-destructive decision?" or "Give me a memory from childhood that explains this adult fear without saying it out loud."

If you're worried about confusing the viewer, you can use visual or tonal cues to differentiate timelines. Costuming, lighting, color palette, or even music can signal the shift. And in the script, clarity is king. Make sure it's always obvious to the reader—and eventually, the audience—when they're watching the past. You can ask ChatGPT, "What's a clean way to transition into a flashback and back again without breaking the flow?" and it'll offer suggestions for slug lines, character action, or visual bridges.

Another technique is the use of unreliable memories. Flashbacks don't have to be objective truth. They can be subjective, twisted by emotion, or even false. A character might remember a moment one way early in the pilot—and then, later, we see the real version. This not only builds suspense but also theme. ChatGPT can help you layer these moments: "Write a version of this flashback where the memory is idealized," then, "Now write the same memory as it really happened." This contrast gives your pilot psychological depth and rewatch value.

And if you're using time shifts to fuel a larger mystery—like a secret identity, hidden betrayal, or lost time—you can ask ChatGPT to help you design the breadcrumbs. Say, "How can I introduce the idea of a lost weekend without giving away the twist?" or "What's a memory fragment I can show that doesn't make sense until the finale?" These moments give your audience something to lean into—and they'll trust you to pay it off later.

Pacing is the final piece of the puzzle. Time shifts slow things down if not managed carefully. You want them to feel like a breath, not a brake. Use ChatGPT to test rhythm: "Where can I place a flashback for emotional impact without stalling the momentum?" or "How can I trim this memory sequence so it lands harder and faster?" When the tempo is right, the emotional payoff hits deeper.

In the end, flashbacks and time shifts are less about style and more about *strategy*. They allow you to control when the audience knows something, how they feel about it, and how it reframes what they've already seen. With ChatGPT helping you test the flow, structure the reveals, and find creative delivery methods, you're not guessing your way through memory—you're wielding it like a scalpel.

Because the past isn't just backstory. It's fuel. And when you introduce it with precision, power, and care, your pilot doesn't just tell a story—it opens a timeline the audience can't wait to unravel.

Writing Characters with Conflicting Objectives

Nothing creates drama faster than putting two characters in a room who both want different things—and won't back down. That's the engine of good television. In a pilot, character conflict isn't just entertaining—it's essential. It defines relationships, raises stakes, creates tension, and fuels your story's forward motion. And the best kind of conflict doesn't come from yelling or violence—it comes from *objective collision*. When one character's goal gets in the way of another's, that's where sparks fly. That's where the audience leans in. And with ChatGPT as your collaborator, you can build those collisions from the ground up—crafting characters with distinct goals, value systems, and personal stakes that make every scene crackle with purpose.

Start with this: every character should want something. Even the side characters. Especially the protagonist. But the real magic happens when two or more characters want things that can't coexist. Maybe one character wants the truth out at any cost, and another wants to bury it to protect someone. Maybe a detective wants justice, and their partner just wants to keep their pension. These are *philosophical collisions* that create instant narrative fuel. With ChatGPT, you can test opposing goals quickly. Say, "Give me two character objectives that would naturally create tension in a workplace drama," and you'll get a foundation you can build on scene by scene.

It helps to think in layers. The surface conflict might be about something external—who gets the promotion, whether to break a rule, how to handle a crisis—but underneath, there's usually a deeper value clash. Ambition vs. loyalty. Justice vs. survival. Order vs. chaos. Ask ChatGPT, "What's a personal value this character holds that could lead to conflict with someone who values community over truth?" and you'll start to create scenes where conflict isn't just situational—it's *inevitable*.

One of the strongest ways to introduce this dynamic in your pilot is through *interruption*. One character's goal is progressing—until someone else steps in and throws it off course. A character is trying to apologize, but someone else hijacks the conversation to deflect blame. A character's about to confess, but someone else interrupts with a crisis that makes honesty dangerous. Ask ChatGPT, "What's a natural interruption that could derail this character's objective in this scene?" and you'll begin constructing drama from purposeful derailment.

These kinds of scenes also create *layers of power*. Who's really in control? Who's pretending to compromise but actually manipulating the situation? One character might seem to be winning the argument—but is actually losing the bigger battle. With ChatGPT, you can explore power shifts by asking, "How can this character subtly gain the upper hand in a conversation without raising their voice?" or "What's a passive-aggressive move that advances this character's goal without open conflict?" This gives your pilot texture, making every line and gesture do narrative work.

It's also worth looking at *mutual objectives that diverge in method*. Maybe two characters both want to save someone—but one wants to call the police and the other wants to break the law. Maybe they both want their company to succeed, but one wants to cut corners and the other wants to do it the right way. These "same destination, different route" scenarios are rich for tension. Ask ChatGPT, "What's a shared goal that would create tension because of different strategies?" and you'll get setups that make characters argue not because they disagree on *what*, but on *how*—which is often more dramatic.

One overlooked approach is to create *emotional objective conflicts*. These are quieter, but just as powerful. One character might want closure, while the other needs distance. One character wants to protect, while the other wants to prove independence. These emotional wants collide in subtle but devastating ways. Ask ChatGPT, "What's an emotional objective that would cause tension between a parent and adult child in a high-stakes setting?" and you'll get relationship fuel that carries weight even when the dialogue is calm.

Once you've designed the conflict, use it to *structure the scene*. Conflict-based scenes are easy to shape: who wants what, who's in the way, and what happens when they push. The moment of collision becomes the dramatic pivot. ChatGPT can help map these scenes out: "Give me a scene outline where one character tries to confess something and another character blocks them without realizing it," or "Write a beat sheet for a scene where both characters escalate their efforts to win." You'll get a working sketch to riff off or refine.

It also helps to make these objectives *impossible to abandon*. A weak objective is easy to drop. A strong one has stakes—personal, moral, or survival-based. That's what keeps the tension alive. You can use ChatGPT to test those stakes: "Why would this character *have* to win this argument, even at a cost?" or "What personal consequence keeps this character fighting when they know they might lose?" High-stakes conflict doesn't have to be loud. It just has to be *inescapable*.

Even scenes that appear cooperative on the surface can be loaded with conflicting objectives. Two friends making plans might be trying to avoid a hard truth. A boss and employee having a calm discussion might each be working from different agendas. Ask ChatGPT, "How can I write this scene so both characters are smiling, but still in conflict?" and you'll learn how to write conflict beneath the surface—which is often the most gripping kind.

In a pilot, these conflicts are golden because they define character relationships right away. They show us who these people are, what they care about, and what they'll do to get it. When objectives clash, characters reveal their values. And values define behavior across a series.

So when you're building scenes in your pilot, don't just ask what happens. Ask: who wants what here? Who's in the way? What won't they give up? And how far are they willing to push?

With ChatGPT helping you brainstorm, test, and refine those objectives, you can create a pilot full of relationships that aren't just dramatic—they're combustible.

And when every scene carries that potential for emotional collision, your audience won't just be watching. They'll be *invested.*

When to Use Voiceover and Internal Monologue

Voiceover and internal monologue can be powerful tools in a television pilot, but they're also tricky. Used well, they invite the audience directly into a character's inner world, adding intimacy, clarity, and even humor. Used poorly, they can feel like lazy storytelling—telling instead of showing, explaining what the visuals should convey, or pulling us out of the moment. The key is to use voiceover with intention. It has to add something the audience *can't* get any other way. And when you're working with ChatGPT, you can experiment with tone, placement, rhythm, and point of view until you find the version that elevates the material instead of weighing it down.

So when should you use it? The best time to consider voiceover or internal monologue is when the internal stakes are as important as the external ones—when the emotional or psychological landscape of a character is a central part of the story. If your protagonist is isolated, conflicted, or lying to everyone around them, internal voiceover can help bridge the gap between how they act and how they really feel. This doesn't mean spelling out their emotions—it means giving us access to the *why* behind their choices. Ask ChatGPT, "What's a revealing internal thought this character could have while pretending everything's fine?" and you'll get authentic, layered material that deepens the moment.

Voiceover is also extremely useful in pilots that are working with complex timelines, worlds, or themes. If your story is nonlinear or set in a world with unusual rules, a short, well-written voiceover can orient the viewer without dragging the story to a halt. Think of the opening of *Dexter*, where voiceover tells us something the visuals never could: that this charming, ordinary-looking guy is a serial killer. Or *Mr. Robot*, where the voiceover reflects the fractured mind of the main character and sets the tone for the entire series. In both cases, the voiceover isn't explaining the plot—it's showing us the character's *lens*. That's what makes it effective.

Another good use is for unreliable narration. If your story is about lies, manipulation, memory, or dual identities, then voiceover gives you a chance to play with truth. A character can say one thing out loud and something totally different in their internal monologue. Or they can tell us one version of the story and then visually contradict it. This kind of tension creates instant suspense and makes the audience feel like they're in on a secret—or questioning everything. Use ChatGPT to brainstorm layered internal lines: "Give me a voiceover that sounds confident but hides insecurity," or "What's a version of this line that suggests the character is lying to themselves?"

Voiceover also works well when your tone is stylized or heightened. In comedies, internal monologue can create contrast between what a character says and what they really think, delivering punchlines or setting up irony. In noir or satire, it can give the show a specific flavor—cynical, poetic, absurd. Ask ChatGPT, "Write a voiceover that makes this sad scene funny through sarcasm," and you'll see how narration can bend tone in interesting directions. When used as a character's personal commentary, it can make even mundane scenes feel vivid.

But the key question is always: *Do I need it?* If your scene works without the voiceover—if the character's emotions are already clear in the visuals, the dialogue, or the acting—then the voiceover might be redundant. You can test this by asking ChatGPT, "Does this voiceover line reveal something the audience wouldn't already know from the scene?" If the answer is no, consider cutting it or rewriting it for more impact.

When writing your pilot, think about the *rules* of voiceover for your show. Is it the protagonist speaking directly to the audience? Are they aware they're doing it? Is it stream-of-consciousness, journal-style, or retrospective? Is it only used in specific situations, like dreams, letters, or therapy? Defining your rules early helps avoid tone confusion later. You can say to ChatGPT, "What are three stylistic approaches to voiceover for a sci-fi drama about memory loss?" and explore different rhythms, tones, and narrative functions.

Another tip is to keep voiceover *tight*. Long chunks of monologue slow pacing, especially early in a pilot when the audience is still trying to get their bearings. Short bursts—one or two sentences—are usually more effective, especially when paired with strong visuals. If you have a paragraph of voiceover, ask ChatGPT, "Trim this voiceover to its emotional essence," and it will help you keep the writing lean and impactful.

Voiceover can also serve as thematic glue. If your series is exploring a big idea—identity, freedom, truth, connection—a recurring internal voice can articulate those ideas in poetic or philosophical ways that aren't natural in spoken dialogue. It becomes the narrator of the soul of the show. ChatGPT can help find that voice. Say, "Give me a voiceover line that expresses the theme of control vs. chaos in a grounded way," and you'll start finding language that frames the series emotionally.

And then there are pilots where voiceover only appears once—right at the beginning or the end—to frame the story or leave us with a haunting final thought. That can be powerful too. A single line of internal monologue to open the show can suggest the tone, the mystery, and the emotional frame in a way that sticks. You can use ChatGPT to experiment: "Write a one-line opening voiceover that hints at the protagonist's dark secret," or "What's a closing voiceover that suggests the story is just beginning?"

Ultimately, voiceover and internal monologue aren't about telling the audience what to think. They're about offering a deeper point of view. They give the audience access—if used with restraint, precision, and style.

So ask yourself: What's the one thing the audience needs to feel—but can't see? What is your character hiding, repressing, or afraid to say out loud? That's where voiceover belongs. And with ChatGPT's help, you can test that voice, explore its tone, shape its rhythm, and make sure it's serving the story—not smothering it.

Because when voiceover works, it doesn't just narrate. It *invites.* It becomes a whisper in the audience's ear, saying, "Come closer. There's more to this story than you think."

Using Visual Metaphors to Deepen the Story

In a medium driven by images, sometimes the most powerful storytelling doesn't come from what's said—but from what's *shown*. Visual metaphors are one of the most subtle, sophisticated tools you can use in a TV pilot to give your story emotional depth, thematic resonance, and a cinematic identity. They aren't just pretty shots or stylistic flourishes. They're *meaning*, wrapped in imagery. When you use them intentionally, you stop telling the audience what your story is about—and start *showing* them in a way that hits harder and lingers longer. And with ChatGPT as your creative partner, you can discover, refine, and strategically place these metaphors so they speak volumes without saying a word.

Let's start with what a visual metaphor actually is. It's an image, object, or physical action that represents something else—usually an emotional truth or thematic idea. A locked door might represent repression. A flickering light might echo a character's uncertain state of mind. A bridge being built or destroyed might symbolize connection or loss. The beauty of visual metaphor is that it works on both a conscious and subconscious level. The audience might not immediately name what it means, but they'll *feel* it.

The best time to start thinking about visual metaphor is before you even write the first scene. What's your show *really* about? Not the plot—but the *theme*. Is it about isolation? Identity? Betrayal? Healing? Ask ChatGPT, "What are visual metaphors that represent abandonment?" or "What physical symbols can reflect the theme of duality?" and you'll start to generate a palette of images that can recur across the episode—and the series.

Now look at your characters. What are they hiding? What are they afraid of? What do they need, deep down? Visual metaphor can help externalize internal conflict. For example, if your protagonist is suppressing grief, maybe they live in a spotless apartment with one locked closet they never open. Or they keep watering a dying plant. Ask ChatGPT, "What's a small action a character might do repeatedly to show they're stuck in the past?" and it'll suggest physical behaviors that can carry emotional weight.

Great pilots often use one or two recurring visual motifs that evolve with the story. Think of it like a visual echo—an image that shows up early in one context and returns later with new meaning. A dripping faucet that begins as background noise but becomes deafening during a character's breakdown. A recurring dream image. A place revisited under different emotional conditions. Ask ChatGPT, "How can I bring back this image in a way that shows the character's growth or decline?" and you'll start building visual story arcs alongside your narrative ones.

Sometimes metaphor lives in *how* you shoot a scene, not just what's in it. Is a character always framed alone in wide shots? Are mirrors used to suggest duality or self-doubt? Is a location always shown from below to suggest oppression—or from above to imply detachment? Ask ChatGPT, "What are some camera angles or framing techniques that reinforce the theme of powerlessness?" and you'll find new ways to let the visuals speak your story's language.

Color is another powerful metaphor. A character who slowly loses color in their wardrobe as their sense of self erodes. A red object that shows up every time someone crosses a moral line. With ChatGPT, you can brainstorm these visual codes: "Suggest a color motif that tracks the emotional decline of the protagonist," and it might give you options that turn wardrobe and set dressing into storytelling tools.

Props can be metaphors, too. An old watch that always runs five minutes slow might symbolize the character's inability to move on. A cracked phone screen might say more about someone's chaotic life than a whole monologue. When used with intention, even mundane objects become part of your narrative vocabulary. Try asking ChatGPT, "What's a common object that could take on symbolic meaning in a story about guilt?" and it might offer ideas you wouldn't have thought of—ideas that can anchor entire scenes.

Nature is another great source of visual metaphor. Weather, animals, landscapes—these can reflect internal states or thematic shifts. A sunny day turning to storm as tensions rise. A stray dog following a character who feels abandoned. A foggy hill they can't see over when they're unsure of their next step. With prompts like, "What's a weather metaphor for emotional confusion?" ChatGPT can help you align the world of your story with its emotional core.

It's important to note that the goal isn't to make the metaphor *obvious*. Subtlety is your friend. You don't want your character to look at a caged bird and say, "I feel trapped, too." You want the audience to *notice* the caged bird and *feel* the connection without being told. That's what makes visual metaphor so elegant—it doesn't interrupt the story, it runs beneath it like an emotional current.

You can also use visual metaphors to tie characters together or show how they differ. Maybe one character always leaves doors open, while another closes everything behind them. One keeps looking up, the other always down. Ask ChatGPT, "What are two contrasting visual habits that show different worldviews between these characters?" and now you're deepening the subtext with every scene.

Even locations can be metaphors. A crumbling school might represent the decay of hope. A pristine but empty mansion could symbolize success without connection. ChatGPT can help generate locations that reinforce character and theme: "Suggest a metaphorical setting for a story about inherited trauma," and it'll offer landscapes and structures that *feel* like the story's emotional terrain.

Finally, the most effective use of visual metaphor in a pilot is *consistency*. Pick one or two strong metaphors and let them evolve. Too many, and you risk muddling the message. But the right image, repeated with purpose and variation, can turn a good pilot into something haunting, memorable, and poetic.

With ChatGPT, you don't have to wait for inspiration to strike. You can test ideas, generate options, and fine-tune the visual language of your show as you go. You can even paste in a scene and ask, "What visual metaphor could I add to this moment to reflect the character's internal shift?" and you'll get thoughtful, symbolic possibilities.

Because in television, the best stories aren't just *told*—they're *seen*. And when you use visual metaphor well, you don't just write a script. You create a world where every image has meaning, every object has weight, and every moment speaks in a language the audience can feel, even before they understand.

Testing Different Opening Scenes with ChatGPT

The opening scene of your pilot is more than just the first few minutes of your story—it's the handshake, the thesis, the promise of what the audience is in for. It sets the tone, introduces the world, hints at the theme, and ideally gives us a reason to keep watching. That's a lot to accomplish in one scene, and it's no surprise that writers often agonize over where to begin. But with ChatGPT as your creative partner, testing multiple versions of your opening becomes less daunting and a whole lot more productive. You don't have to commit to one idea right away. Instead, you can run scenarios, test emotional impact, try different genres or tones, and find the one that *feels right*—quickly, clearly, and without starting over each time.

Let's say you already know your story. You've got a great premise, compelling characters, and a solid outline. But you're not sure whether to start with a flash-forward to the climax, a quiet character moment, or a dramatic scene in media res. This is where ChatGPT becomes your development sandbox. You can prompt it with: "Give me three different versions of an opening scene for a drama about a former detective haunted by a cold case," and you'll get three distinct takes—maybe one atmospheric and slow-burning, one punchy and action-packed, and one quiet and reflective. You can compare how they land emotionally, how they frame the protagonist, and how much narrative tension they create.

Each opening version might emphasize a different aspect of your story. One might highlight the theme. Another might lean into world-building. A third might start with pure mystery. ChatGPT helps you isolate and amplify these options. Ask, "Write an opening scene that introduces the show's central mystery without giving away the twist," or "Write a scene that introduces the protagonist through action rather than dialogue," and you'll begin to discover what kind of opener best supports the heart of your show.

If your show plays with genre, tone, or structure, testing openings becomes even more critical. Let's say your story is a sci-fi thriller with comedic undertones. You can ask ChatGPT, "Write this opening scene as a dry comedy, then rewrite it with a suspenseful tone," and you'll immediately see how tone changes everything—from dialogue to pacing to visual cues. This process lets you calibrate your opening so it reflects the series you actually want to make—not the one you imagined before you saw it on the page.

You can also explore how much to tell the audience. Do you start with a big mystery, or do you ground them in character first? Try prompting ChatGPT with, "Write an opening where the viewer knows more than the protagonist," then, "Now write it where the protagonist knows something the audience doesn't." Each version creates a different kind of tension. You might find one builds curiosity, while the other builds suspense.

Some of the strongest pilots open with a question. Something visual, emotional, or character-driven that the audience wants answered. ChatGPT is great at helping you find that question. You can say, "What's an opening image that asks a compelling question about identity or trust?" or "Give me a scenario that hooks the viewer without needing any exposition." The goal isn't to explain—it's to *intrigue.*

Let's say you're choosing between starting the pilot with a voiceover, a dream sequence, or a direct jump into action. With ChatGPT, you can write all three versions side-by-side, compare how they sound, how they feel, and how they transition into the next beat. Try something like, "Give me a one-minute cold open for a thriller, followed by the same scene told from a flashback structure." You'll quickly get a sense of what clicks—and what feels forced.

ChatGPT also helps you get unstuck. Maybe you've written a version of your opening scene, but it feels flat. You can paste it in and say, "How can I raise the stakes in this opening?" or "What visual element could make this opening feel more symbolic or eerie?" It might suggest a background detail, a sound cue, a character reaction, or a new conflict that electrifies the scene.

And once you land on a version you like, you can take it even further. Ask ChatGPT, "How does this opening set up the character arc for the pilot?" or "What thematic threads does this opening suggest, and how can I carry those into later scenes?" You're not just testing the scene—you're pressure-testing its *purpose*. The best opening scenes aren't isolated—they ripple through the entire episode.

You can also use ChatGPT to predict audience reactions. Say, "How would this scene read to someone watching without knowing anything about the series?" or "Does this opening raise a clear dramatic question?" You'll get reader feedback without waiting on coverage, which helps you revise faster and with more confidence.

Even after you've settled on your favorite version, keep the others. Alternate openings often become flashbacks, midseason cold opens, or parallel storylines later in the show. Just because you don't use it now doesn't mean it's wasted. In fact, having tested those options makes your pilot feel *intentional*. It's been chosen—not guessed.

The bottom line is this: your pilot only gets one shot to grab the audience. But you don't have to find the perfect opening on your first try. You can explore, play, test, tweak—and with ChatGPT's speed and flexibility, that process becomes creative instead of frustrating.

So don't wait for lightning to strike. Try that quiet character beat. Try that shocking image. Try the memory, the murder, the metaphor, the mislead. Let the opening scene become a lab for the *best possible version of your show*.

Because when the audience presses play, they're asking one question: "Is this worth my time?" And your opening scene—crafted with intention, curiosity, and clarity—has the power to make them stay for the whole ride.

How to Structure a Multi-Protagonist Series

Writing a series with more than one protagonist isn't just about juggling screen time—it's about crafting a balanced narrative where every lead character feels essential to the story. Whether you're writing a sprawling crime drama, an ensemble comedy, a dystopian thriller, or a small-town mystery, multi-protagonist storytelling opens up incredible possibilities for depth, tension, and emotional resonance. But it also adds complexity. You're not just tracking one arc—you're weaving several together so they resonate individually *and* as a whole. Luckily, with ChatGPT at your side, you can develop and test each protagonist's journey, interlink their stories, and build a structure that feels seamless rather than scattered.

The first step is knowing *why* your story needs multiple protagonists. Each character should offer a unique lens on the world, theme, or conflict of the show. Maybe one is an insider while the other is an outsider. Maybe they're rivals, allies, or completely unaware of each other—at first. What matters is that each storyline matters. If you can remove a character's thread and the pilot still works, then they're not truly a protagonist—they're supporting. Ask ChatGPT, "What's a reason to tell this story through three main characters instead of one?" and it will help you identify the function and weight of each point of view.

Next, think about how their stories intersect—or don't. Some multi-protagonist shows, like *Game of Thrones*, keep characters in separate locations and storylines for long stretches, only occasionally overlapping. Others, like *Stranger Things*, weave characters in and out of each other's plots constantly. Both approaches work—but the structure changes depending on how interconnected the lives are. ChatGPT can help you map this: "Outline a pilot where three protagonists start separately but end up crossing paths by the final scene," or "Structure a story where each character's arc reveals a different piece of a larger mystery."

Now let's talk about balance. You don't necessarily need to give equal screen time to every protagonist in every episode—but they should each have a clear arc, want something, face obstacles, and change or make a choice by the end of the pilot. Otherwise, the audience won't connect. If one character's plot is clearly driving the story, consider framing the others as orbiting characters who come into sharper focus in later episodes. Use ChatGPT to test this: "How can I shift the spotlight between characters in a way that keeps all their stories emotionally engaging?"

When planning your pilot, it's helpful to outline each protagonist's journey separately. Break down their story beats, emotional arcs, turning points, and revelations. Then look at how these threads overlap, echo each other, or contrast. ChatGPT is great for this kind of structural thinking. Ask, "Give me a parallel scene structure for two protagonists whose choices mirror each other," or "What's a plot device that can link three unrelated characters by the midpoint of the pilot?"

One effective structure for multi-protagonist shows is the *braid*. You open with one character, then cut to another, then a third, and slowly braid their arcs together—either thematically or through literal contact. The viewer begins to understand how the stories relate by the rhythm of the edit, the transitions, or the shared tension. You can ask ChatGPT, "Help me structure a braided narrative for four characters with a common past but different present goals," and you'll get a draft roadmap that keeps each thread compelling while building toward convergence.

Tone is especially important in this kind of structure. If each protagonist has a wildly different tone—one dark and brooding, one quirky and comedic, one grounded and realistic—the audience can feel whiplash. That doesn't mean you can't have contrast, but you'll want a unifying visual or emotional aesthetic. Use ChatGPT to help align tone: "How can

I make a political drama and a romantic subplot feel like they belong in the same show?" or "Suggest transitions that can shift tone between two protagonists without losing cohesion."

Your theme is the glue. If your show is about identity, then every protagonist's story should explore identity in a different way. If it's about truth, then maybe each character is hiding something—or chasing a different version of the truth. Ask ChatGPT, "How can each of these protagonists explore a different facet of the theme of power?" and you'll find ways to unify their arcs without forcing them into the same plot.

In the pilot specifically, think about how you introduce each protagonist. Do you give each of them a mini-cold open before the title card? Do you start with one and meet the others as the story unfolds? Do you begin in one protagonist's world and let the others collide with it? These choices determine pacing, audience attachment, and narrative clarity. You can explore multiple versions with ChatGPT: "Give me three ways to introduce four protagonists in a one-hour pilot," and weigh the pros and cons of each structure.

Remember, even if the protagonists are introduced separately, the audience needs to feel a promise that their stories will matter to each other eventually. You're not writing four separate shows—you're building one tapestry. That could mean shared enemies, intersecting backstories, or parallel dilemmas. You might not reveal all the connections in the pilot, but you want to plant the sense that something is *pulling them together*.

Also, be careful with overload. Don't try to tell four complete stories in one hour. Focus on introducing each protagonist with clarity and conflict. Give them a strong want, a compelling obstacle, and a reason for the audience to care. The deeper backstories, long-term arcs, and secondary characters can come in future episodes. ChatGPT can help you prioritize: "Which beats are essential to establish a protagonist in a pilot, and which can wait until episode two?"

And finally, let each protagonist shine in their own emotional space. One might drive the plot. Another might carry the theme. A third might deliver levity or mystery. When each one feels distinct, vital, and emotionally alive, your pilot becomes more than an introduction—it becomes a world we want to stay in, with people we're eager to follow. With ChatGPT helping you test ideas, simulate scenes, map arcs, and balance structure, you don't have to juggle all these protagonists alone. You can build a layered, dynamic series where multiple leads don't compete for attention—they *elevate* each other.

Because in the best multi-protagonist series, every character is the star of their own story. And the magic comes when all those stars start to orbit the same sky.

Choosing a Style: Single-Camera or Multi-Cam Writing

Before you write a single line of your TV pilot, one of the most important creative choices you'll make is deciding whether your show is a single-camera or a multi-camera production. This decision isn't just technical—it fundamentally affects how your story is told, how your scenes are structured, how your characters speak, and even how the audience experiences the world you're building. It's the style, the rhythm, the language of your show. And while some writers dive straight into the script and figure this out later, choosing early gives you clarity, confidence, and creative focus. The good news is, with ChatGPT, you can test both formats and explore the storytelling potential of each before committing to a direction.

Let's break down the basics. A **single-camera** show is shot like a movie—one camera capturing each shot, often with cinematic lighting, location shooting, and a range of visual storytelling tools. Think *Breaking Bad*, *The Office*, *Atlanta*, *Stranger Things*, *Fleabag*. Single-cam lets you get intimate, dramatic, surreal, or visually stylized. You can use flashbacks, time jumps, quick cuts, visual metaphors, and silence as storytelling devices. The tone can shift quickly, the settings can vary wildly, and the humor can come from awkward moments or subtle glances rather than punchlines.

A **multi-cam** show is filmed in front of a live studio audience (or with a laugh track), using multiple cameras shooting simultaneously from fixed positions. It's more like theater—performers hit their marks, deliver lines to the audience, and reset for the next scene. Think *Friends*, *The Big Bang Theory*, *Two and a Half Men*, *Mom*, *Frasier*. Multi-cam thrives on rhythm. Dialogue is tighter, punchlines land harder, and there's a constant back-and-forth energy that works especially well for character-driven comedy with strong setups and payoffs.

If you're unsure which to choose, ChatGPT is an excellent tool for helping you experiment. Take a basic scene—say, two characters arguing in a coffee shop—and ask ChatGPT to write it in both single-cam and multi-cam styles. The single-cam version might focus on subtle reactions, awkward silences, and jump cuts to flashbacks. The multi-cam version might tighten the dialogue into zingers, build up to a big laugh, and structure the argument with clean reversals and callbacks. By comparing them, you'll get an instant feel for what suits your voice, your story, and your tone.

Tone really is the deciding factor. Is your show grounded, introspective, or visually stylized? Single-cam probably fits. Is it joke-driven, character-based, and rhythmically comedic? Then multi-cam might be your home. Ask ChatGPT, "How would the tone of this family sitcom change if written as a single-cam versus a multi-cam?" and it'll break down the shift in pacing, dialogue, and structure for you.

Setting also plays a role. Multi-cam tends to rely on a few core sets—apartments, coffee shops, offices—because of the studio setup. If your show needs lots of locations, single-cam is more flexible. But that doesn't mean you can't stretch the format. Shows like *How I Met Your Mother* pushed the limits of multi-cam with creative cutaways, while single-cams like *Brooklyn Nine-Nine* use quick edits and musical cues to mimic multi-cam pacing. ChatGPT can help you find that middle ground if you want to blend tones: "How can I write a visually dynamic show with the humor style of a multi-cam sitcom?"

Writing-wise, multi-cam scripts have tighter stage directions, faster scene changes, and punchier dialogue. They often follow a clear A-plot/B-plot structure with big beats and defined act breaks. Single-cam scripts allow for more naturalistic dialogue, offbeat pacing, and smaller emotional moments. They're also freer in terms of format—you can include montages, visual gags, or long silences with a single line of direction. If you're torn, ask ChatGPT to convert one of your scenes: "Rewrite this scene from a single-camera drama as a multi-cam sitcom scene," and it will help you see how jokes, pacing, and tone shift across formats.

One overlooked consideration is **audience experience**. Multi-cam shows are designed to feel communal. The laughs cue the audience emotionally. It feels warm, familiar, and performative. Single-cam shows often feel more introspective or cinematic—like you're peering into someone's private world rather than watching a show being performed. ChatGPT can help you test this too: "What's the emotional impact difference between a single-cam breakup scene and a multi-cam one?" and you'll start to see how the format actually changes the *meaning* of moments.

There's also the **writing process** itself. Multi-cam shows are usually written in writers' rooms, heavily rewritten based on table reads and audience reactions. Jokes are tested live, and rewrites are rapid. Single-cam writing is often more director-driven, with more visual planning and mood control. If you're planning to write and produce something independently or on a small team, single-cam might give you more flexibility. If you're aiming for a traditional network comedy, multi-cam still has a strong place.

If you're building a series bible or pitch document, identifying the format clearly helps sell the show. Networks and producers want to know what kind of series you're writing, how it will look, feel, and *sound*. You can use ChatGPT to help build out that pitch language. Say, "Write a paragraph explaining why this workplace comedy is best suited for a multi-camera format," and it'll give you a concise justification you can drop into your materials.

At the end of the day, the decision between single-cam and multi-cam should support the kind of story you're trying to tell. Let the tone, structure, characters, and emotional heartbeat of the show guide the choice. Then let ChatGPT help you test, shape, and fully embrace that style across your scenes, your dialogue, and your entire storytelling approach.

Because once you commit to the format, everything gets clearer. The jokes land sharper. The drama hits deeper. And your pilot starts to sound and feel like the show it was always meant to be.

Building Momentum from Scene to Scene

One of the biggest challenges in writing a pilot—especially one you're trying to complete in a single day—is keeping the energy alive. Every scene you write has to lead naturally into the next, carrying the audience forward without confusion, hesitation, or drop in interest. This flow, this drive, is what we call narrative momentum. It's not just about fast pacing or non-stop action—it's about creating a continuous pull that makes viewers feel like they can't look away. When each scene sets up a question, a conflict, or a need that the next scene answers or escalates, your story starts to roll downhill with power and purpose. And when you're working with ChatGPT, you can build and test that momentum as you go, refining each transition until your pilot feels like a ride the audience doesn't want to get off.

A scene in isolation can be beautifully written, but if it doesn't push the story or character forward—or link clearly to what comes next—it risks stalling your narrative. That's why momentum isn't just about what happens inside a scene. It's about how that scene *connects* to the next one. You can use ChatGPT to make those connections stronger. For example, paste in two consecutive scenes and ask, "Does Scene Two feel like a natural consequence of Scene One?" or "How can I rewrite the transition between these scenes to feel more urgent or fluid?" This kind of testing helps you identify and fix weak links in your chain.

One simple but powerful way to build momentum is to always end a scene with a hook. That hook can be a question, a new discovery, a decision, a twist, or a literal action that demands a response. Ask ChatGPT, "What's a strong ending beat for this scene that creates anticipation for what comes next?" You'll get suggestions like a character discovering a secret, receiving a mysterious message, or walking into a room they weren't supposed to enter. The goal is to make the audience ask, "What now?" and then answer that question in the very next beat.

Momentum also comes from escalation. Each scene should either raise the stakes, deepen the emotional tension, or complicate the situation. If a character starts the scene with a problem, they should end it with a bigger one—or a new version of the same one. You can prompt ChatGPT with, "How can this scene raise the stakes from the previous one without repeating the same beat?" and explore versions that keep the tension rising instead of circling.

Don't underestimate character momentum, either. It's not just about plot moving forward—it's about people being changed by what's happening. After each scene, ask: has the character made a new choice, discovered something, or faced a new obstacle? You can ask ChatGPT, "What is the emotional shift in this scene, and how does it change the character's next move?" This ensures your story isn't just moving—it's evolving.

Sometimes momentum is about rhythm. If you have a heavy dialogue scene, follow it with action or movement. If you've just had an emotionally intense moment, maybe follow it with something that brings levity or clarity. Contrast keeps the momentum from going flat. Ask ChatGPT, "What's a good tonal shift after this emotionally heavy scene that still fits the overall story?" and you'll get beats that offer breath without breaking flow.

Another key to keeping momentum alive is cause and effect. Each scene should exist *because* of the last. If you can move a scene around in the order of the script without affecting anything, it probably doesn't belong. Use ChatGPT to pressure-test this by saying, "What's the cause-and-effect link between these two scenes?" or "Does this scene feel like a logical next step based on what just happened?" You'll see clearly whether your story is a chain or just a collection of events.

When writing multiple storylines—as you often do in a pilot—it's important to keep each thread moving even when you cut away. ChatGPT can help you plan this out: "How can I structure the B-plot so it escalates in parallel with the

A-plot?" or "What's a good beat to cut away on that will make viewers eager to return to this subplot?" You don't want any storyline to feel like filler or a detour.

Momentum also benefits from anticipation. Set up something in one scene that pays off a few scenes later. It could be a loaded line of dialogue, a visual clue, or a character acting out of sync. These little setups act like narrative breadcrumbs that the audience follows without even realizing it. You can ask ChatGPT, "What's a small moment in Scene Two that could pay off in Scene Six?" and begin layering your script with satisfying callbacks and reveals.

And then there's pacing—the tempo of your script. Momentum doesn't always mean fast. It means *deliberate*. If every scene is high energy, the audience gets exhausted. If every scene is slow, they lose interest. Use ChatGPT to find the rhythm: "Help me alternate scene lengths and types to create a balanced narrative flow," or "Suggest a calmer character moment that still adds tension to the story." Think of your pilot as a piece of music—build, release, build again.

A smart move is to outline momentum before writing. Ask ChatGPT, "Map out the tension level of each major beat in my pilot," and it'll help you visualize when your story rises, plateaus, or dips. If you see too many flat points in a row, it's time to restructure.

And finally, keep the big picture in mind. The goal of your pilot is to launch the series—not just tell a complete story, but to *promise* many more. Your final scene should leave your audience with momentum not just toward the next scene—but toward the next *episode*. Ask ChatGPT, "How can I end this pilot on a beat that drives the story forward into episode two?" and you'll craft a closing moment that doesn't just land—it propels.

Momentum isn't about writing faster. It's about *writing forward*. Every choice, every beat, every scene should pull us deeper into the world, closer to the characters, and farther along the story.

Because in the world of television, momentum is trust. When the audience feels you're guiding them somewhere compelling, they'll follow—scene by scene, episode by episode, all the way to the very end.

Dialoguing Between Character and Theme

At the heart of every great television pilot lies a conversation—not just between characters, but between characters and the *theme* of the story. When the dialogue in your pilot not only drives plot and reveals personality, but also subtly explores the big questions your show is asking, you've created something special. Characters aren't just talking to each other—they're talking to the heart of your narrative. They're pushing and pulling on the thematic threads that tie your story together. And with ChatGPT as your creative ally, you can test, explore, and sharpen that conversation until your dialogue not only sounds great, but *means* something deeper.

Theme isn't something you announce in bold letters. It's the question your story keeps asking. Is loyalty worth the cost? Can people really change? What's the price of truth? Whatever your core theme is, your characters should embody different viewpoints about it—whether they know it or not. And that tension should live in the dialogue. The arguments they have, the jokes they make, the secrets they keep—all of it becomes a way to examine the theme from multiple angles.

The first step is knowing what your theme *is*. Not just broadly, like "love" or "justice," but what specific angle you're exploring. "Can you love someone without trusting them?" or "Is justice real, or just the illusion of power?" Once you have that thematic spine, you can start to figure out how each character relates to it. ChatGPT can help you map this out. Ask, "How do these three characters reflect different perspectives on the theme of control versus freedom?" and you'll get a breakdown that becomes the foundation for how they speak, argue, and relate to each other.

Let's say your theme is "truth versus self-preservation." You might have one character who always tells the truth no matter what, one who hides it to protect others, and one who lies to protect themselves. Now imagine all three in a scene, debating something as simple as whether to report a mistake at work. The scene suddenly becomes more than plot—it becomes a thematic exploration in miniature. Ask ChatGPT, "Write a dialogue where each character reveals their stance on truth without directly stating it," and you'll get layered subtext instead of heavy-handed exposition.

Subtext is key here. You don't want your characters giving TED Talks on your theme. You want their point of view to *leak* into their words—their tone, their metaphors, their frustrations. A character might say, "Rules are for people who can't think for themselves," and we understand that their relationship to power and authority is going to be different from someone who says, "Without rules, everything falls apart." These aren't random lines—they're thematic reflections.

When you write with ChatGPT, you can pressure-test your dialogue for this kind of depth. Paste in a scene and ask, "Does this dialogue reflect the show's core theme?" or "How can I rewrite this conversation to better highlight the tension between hope and cynicism?" The AI can suggest tweaks, reversals, or entirely new beats that sharpen your character's role in the thematic conversation.

Theme can also shape *what* your characters talk about. Small talk, jokes, insults, and compliments can all be colored by worldview. If your theme is about connection versus isolation, then even a scene about ordering coffee can reveal something. One character chats with the barista, the other stares at their phone. One sees every interaction as meaningful, the other as transactional. You can ask ChatGPT, "How would two characters with opposite views on connection order lunch together?" and get a short scene that turns the mundane into a statement.

Even silences can be thematic. A character who refuses to answer a direct question is often speaking louder than one who says too much. If your story is about repression, trauma, or denial, silence becomes a character choice—and a thematic one. Ask ChatGPT, "How can I show a character's fear of vulnerability through dialogue avoidance?" and you'll discover that not talking *is* a kind of talking when it comes to theme.

Monologues and soliloquies are another chance to lean into theme—but they need to feel earned and grounded. You don't want your character to suddenly become the voice of the writer. Instead, let the moment grow from the character's struggle. Maybe they're trying to justify something, or trying to convince themselves of something they're not sure about. ChatGPT can help shape this: "Write an internal monologue that explores the theme of redemption from a character who doesn't believe they deserve it." You'll get something raw, conflicted, and thematic without being preachy.

Theme can also evolve through dialogue across the pilot. Maybe a character begins with a firm belief, and scene by scene, they're challenged—by others, by events, by themselves. Their dialogue becomes the record of that internal shift. Ask ChatGPT, "Track a shift in theme-related dialogue across three key scenes where a character's belief is tested," and you'll get a sense of how conversation builds transformation.

One of the most dynamic ways to handle theme is through conflict. Characters who care about different things will fight—and their fights are full of theme. Ask ChatGPT, "Write a heated argument between two characters with opposing values about survival and sacrifice," and you'll get a scene that doesn't just move the plot forward, it exposes the emotional and philosophical heart of your show.

Don't forget humor, either. Jokes can carry thematic weight. Sarcasm, dark humor, even absurdity—these can all be tools to explore how characters deflect, confront, or ridicule the ideas your story is about. "Write banter that reflects two characters' differing views on success," and you might get a tone-perfect exchange that's both funny and meaningful.

When you dialogue between character and theme, you're giving your pilot a soul. You're making every scene matter on more than one level. The surface might be about getting a job, breaking into a house, or going on a date—but underneath, it's about the very things that make us human.

With ChatGPT, you can keep asking the right questions, pushing your characters further, deepening their contradictions, and sharpening their voices until your script isn't just a story—it's a conversation the audience wants to keep listening to.

Because when characters speak with purpose, and every line echoes the larger questions your series is asking, your pilot doesn't just entertain. It *resonates.*

Getting Feedback from ChatGPT Before Others Do

One of the most powerful and underused aspects of writing a pilot with ChatGPT is using it not just as your writing partner, but as your *first audience*. Before you send your draft to friends, colleagues, or professional readers—before you even commit to certain scenes or structure—ChatGPT can give you early, honest, helpful feedback that strengthens your work and builds your confidence. You don't have to wait days or weeks for someone to read your script. You can test your ideas, scenes, dialogue, and pacing in real-time, on your own terms, and with no judgment. It's like having a development exec, script editor, and fellow screenwriter sitting across the table, available 24/7.

Most writers dread feedback because it comes with emotional risk. You worry about sounding amateur. You worry about losing your voice. You worry someone will tear apart something you worked hard on. With ChatGPT, that pressure disappears. You're free to explore, make mistakes, fix issues, and try again—all before a single person sees your script. It becomes a safe zone where your creative process gets smarter, faster, and more fearless.

The simplest place to start is scene review. You can paste in a scene and ask, "Does this scene accomplish what it needs to emotionally?" or "Is this dialogue carrying the conflict clearly?" ChatGPT will highlight strengths and gently suggest areas for improvement. It might notice if a character's motivation isn't clear, if the pacing feels off, or if the tone shifts awkwardly. You're not guessing what works—you're getting real-time insight that helps you revise with precision.

You can go even deeper by asking for a reader's perspective. Try prompts like, "Read this like a producer considering whether to greenlight the series. What stands out? What's missing?" or "What would an actor love or struggle with in this scene?" or even "What impression would this scene leave on a first-time viewer?" These kinds of targeted feedback sessions give you angles you may not have considered, and help you shape your script for the people who matter most in the process—audiences, readers, and collaborators.

Feedback on structure is another huge advantage. You can drop in an outline or a beat sheet and ask, "Is the midpoint strong enough?" or "Does the climax of the pilot deliver on the setup in Act One?" ChatGPT can quickly walk you through cause-and-effect, emotional payoff, character arc development, and more. You can test different structural changes before you even write them: "What would happen if I moved this reveal earlier?" or "If I made this character's secret public in Act Two, how would that affect the pacing?" These what-if tests help you refine your plot before you waste time writing a version that doesn't quite click.

One incredibly useful feature is dialogue analysis. You can paste a scene and say, "Does each character sound distinct?" or "Is this line too on-the-nose?" or "How can I make this exchange sharper without losing the subtext?" ChatGPT will suggest revisions, identify clichés, and even help you write more in a character's voice. You can ask, "Make this line more emotionally conflicted," or "Add tension between the lines," and it will return dialogue that does more heavy lifting without being heavy-handed.

Tone consistency is another area where ChatGPT shines. Maybe your show is meant to blend humor and heartbreak, or mix genre with grounded realism. You can say, "Does the tone of this scene match the rest of the pilot?" or "Does this emotional beat feel earned given the tone I've set up?" ChatGPT can help you iron out tonal inconsistencies that might jar or confuse your audience—and suggest language or rhythm adjustments to get things back on track.

Theme alignment is another powerful form of feedback you can get early. Ask, "Does this scene reflect the theme of identity and deception?" or "How could this beat echo the show's central idea of second chances?" and ChatGPT will help you make sure your story is speaking in harmony with its deeper meaning. That's the kind of polish that turns a decent script into something people connect with.

One of the most useful ways to use ChatGPT for feedback is to play devil's advocate against your own choices. Say, "What's the argument for *cutting* this scene?" or "What's a reason this character might not belong in the pilot?" You'll get a list of objections that you can either address or refute in the script itself, strengthening your vision. You're not undermining your work—you're pressure-testing it so you can defend every creative decision with confidence.

And when you're nearing the finish line, ChatGPT can help simulate a table read. Ask it to "Read this scene aloud with clear character transitions," and you'll get a rhythm of how the dialogue plays. You'll notice where the lines drag, where the energy spikes, or where the pacing dips. You can even say, "Pretend you're a showrunner reading this cold—what stands out?" or "What's the most memorable image or line from this scene?" and you'll begin to understand your script from the outside in.

Getting feedback from ChatGPT isn't about replacing human readers—it's about *preparing* for them. By the time you send your script to a writer's group, an agent, a showrunner, or a friend, you've already had the difficult conversations. You've already examined the weak spots, clarified the themes, tested the pacing, sharpened the dialogue, and dialed in the tone. The feedback you get from others will be more advanced, more specific, and less about fixing fundamentals—because you've already done that work here.

And best of all, this feedback loop never closes. You can rewrite a scene and instantly test it again. You can brainstorm alternatives without fear. You can ask hard questions, get detailed answers, and move forward without stalling.

Because writing a pilot is a process—and ChatGPT is your best tool for making that process faster, smarter, and more creatively rewarding before anyone else even gets to read it.

Creating Emotional Arcs in Just One Episode

A great pilot doesn't just introduce characters, settings, and story—it makes us *feel* something. And not just once, but all the way through. Even though your characters will (hopefully) evolve across an entire season or series, your pilot should still contain complete emotional arcs—especially for your main character. These arcs give the episode structure, resonance, and momentum. When a character starts in one emotional place and ends in another, it leaves the audience with a sense of closure and curiosity. They feel like something happened *inside* the character, not just around them. With ChatGPT as your creative co-writer, you can track, test, and fine-tune those arcs with precision and speed.

Think of the emotional arc as the *inside story*. The plot is what happens to your character; the emotional arc is how it affects them. If your pilot's external story is about someone trying to get their job back, the internal story might be about rebuilding their self-worth. If it's about solving a mystery, it might also be about regaining trust. You can use ChatGPT to help define these layers by asking, "What's an emotional journey that parallels this character's external goal?" or "What inner change could mirror the plot twist in Act Two?"

The key to building an emotional arc in one episode is to give the character an emotional *starting point*. This is where they begin, emotionally or psychologically. They might be afraid of commitment, in denial, angry, guarded, lonely, overconfident, or stuck. Then, over the course of the episode, challenge that emotional state. The plot should push them into situations that confront their flaw or wound. Ask ChatGPT, "What kind of external event would challenge this character's emotional armor?" and it will help you find a compelling situation that forces growth.

Once you've got the starting point, think about what moment in the episode marks the *turning point*. This is when the character is forced to confront something within themselves. It doesn't mean they fully change—they just start to *see* the thing they've been avoiding. Maybe they break down after pretending to be fine. Maybe they lash out at the wrong person. Maybe they admit something they never wanted to say out loud. You can say to ChatGPT, "What's a scene that would crack this character emotionally without making it melodramatic?" and you'll get moments that ring true rather than feel forced.

The ending beat is where the arc lands. It's not about resolving everything. It's about suggesting that something inside the character has shifted. If they were emotionally closed off, maybe they finally return a call they've been avoiding. If they were angry, maybe they stop fighting for a second. You can use ChatGPT to help shape that moment: "What's a subtle but clear emotional beat to end this episode on, showing growth without being too neat?"

Some pilots use **mirrored scenes** to show emotional change. The character might do something at the beginning, and do it again differently at the end. Maybe they walk into a room with swagger at the start—and limp out of the same room with quiet humility by the end. ChatGPT can help you build those echoes: "What's a scene I can repeat at the end to show the character has changed?"

Dialogue is another great tool for emotional arc development. A character might repeat a phrase, but change its meaning. Or they might finally say something they couldn't earlier in the episode. These moments give the audience a feeling of transformation. Ask ChatGPT, "What's a line this character could say at the start, and then again at the end with different emotional weight?" and you'll get rich dialogue that tracks growth.

Emotional arcs don't have to be dramatic. A small change can carry huge weight. A character who was disengaged finally leans in. A loner sits with someone for a moment longer than necessary. These are the kinds of beats that stick with an audience. And they make the pilot feel like a complete story, not just a setup. ChatGPT can help you mine those small beats: "What's a quiet emotional action that signals this character is beginning to trust again?"

In ensemble shows, not every character needs a full emotional arc in the pilot. But your central protagonist should. Supporting characters can have mini-arcs or emotional beats that tease who they'll become later. You can test this by asking, "Which of these supporting characters could have a satisfying micro-arc in this episode?" ChatGPT will help you balance the emotional landscape of your cast.

Emotional arcs also create *momentum*. When a character feels something deeply, the audience wants to see what they'll do next. That means your emotional beats aren't just internal—they push the plot forward. Use ChatGPT to help align the internal and external stories: "How can this character's emotional turning point drive the next plot beat?"

One final trick is to give your protagonist an emotional *lie* they believe at the start. Something like, "I'm better off alone," or "Nobody can be trusted," or "Success is all that matters." Then, over the course of the episode, challenge that lie. You don't have to fully debunk it—but make it crack. Make them question it. Ask ChatGPT, "What's an emotional lie this character believes, and what's a moment that starts to unravel it?" That one answer could give your whole pilot emotional shape.

In the end, emotional arcs give your story *weight*. They make your pilot feel like more than just exposition or plot mechanics. They make it feel *alive*. When the audience sees someone change—even just a little—they lean in. They relate. They root for more.

And when you use ChatGPT to guide, map, and test those arcs, you don't have to write from instinct alone. You can build emotional journeys that are intentional, resonant, and beautifully woven into the DNA of your story.

Because a good plot makes a show *interesting*. But a strong emotional arc? That's what makes it unforgettable.

Rewriting Scenes for More Punch

The first draft of a scene is where you discover the bones. It's functional—it gets the characters from point A to point B, it delivers the basic beats, and maybe it even has a decent line or two. But when a scene lacks punch, it just sort of sits there. It might not be *bad*, but it doesn't demand attention. It doesn't stay with the viewer. That's where the rewrite comes in. Rewriting for punch means sharpening the emotional beats, tightening the rhythm, enhancing the tension, raising the stakes, and making the scene *feel alive*. And with ChatGPT as your scene doctor on call, you can revise, test, and elevate your writing quickly and fearlessly—turning flat into fire, good into great.

Start by identifying why a scene feels dull. Is it too long? Is it missing conflict? Is the dialogue too on-the-nose or too vague? Is the pacing dragging, or does it feel like nothing changes from beginning to end? You can copy and paste the scene into ChatGPT and ask, "What's not working about this scene?" or "Where does the energy drop here?" and you'll get a breakdown of weak points—plus suggestions on how to tighten, cut, or add heat.

A common issue with first drafts is **passive characters**. They're talking, maybe reacting, but they're not *doing* much. A punchier rewrite often starts by making the characters more active. Who wants what in this moment? Who's pushing forward and who's resisting? You can ask ChatGPT, "How can I make this character more assertive in this scene?" or "What action could this character take that raises the stakes right now?" The scene gets punchier the moment someone makes a bold move or a risky choice.

Another fix is **heightening the conflict**. Even quiet scenes need tension—emotional, ideological, relational. If everyone's agreeing or just exchanging information, you're probably losing momentum. Ask ChatGPT, "How can I turn this calm conversation into a power struggle?" or "What hidden conflict could be bubbling beneath this dialogue?" It might suggest an old grudge, a secret, or even a subtle tone shift that puts one character off balance. That shift is where the punch lives.

Dialogue is one of the fastest ways to add punch. Look at each line and ask: is this the most interesting way this character could say this? Could it be shorter? Sharper? More revealing? More confrontational? Less polite? You can say to ChatGPT, "Make this dialogue more combative," or "Give this line a darker edge," or "Add a sarcastic twist to this exchange," and it'll provide alternatives that often spark your own revisions. Dialogue gets punchy when it's unexpected, loaded with subtext, or rhythmically snappy.

Cutting fat is another underrated superpower. Sometimes a scene lacks punch simply because it's too padded. There's setup you don't need, or exposition you've already said elsewhere. Try asking ChatGPT, "Trim this scene by 30% without losing the core emotion," and you'll get a leaner, faster, cleaner version that probably feels more urgent. Don't be afraid to be ruthless—brevity forces your lines and actions to carry more weight.

Punch also comes from **surprise**. What happens in the scene that the audience didn't expect? Maybe a character reveals a truth, takes an action, or explodes in emotion. Ask ChatGPT, "What twist could I add to this scene to shift the power dynamic?" or "How could this scene end on a surprising note that raises the stakes for the next one?" Even a subtle change in a character's expression or a beat of silence can add tension if it comes at just the right moment.

You can also build punch through **visual detail**. A rewrite isn't just about the lines—it's about what we *see*. Is there a strong image? Is the blocking doing any storytelling? Can the setting or props reinforce the scene's emotional energy? Try asking ChatGPT, "What visual element could underscore the theme of betrayal in this scene?" or "How can I use the setting to make this moment feel more claustrophobic?" The right visual cue can turn a flat room into a pressure cooker.

Another tip is to **amplify the stakes**. What does each character stand to lose or gain in this moment? If it's unclear, the scene will lack urgency. Ask ChatGPT, "How can I raise the emotional stakes of this confrontation?" or "What would make this decision feel more dangerous for the protagonist?" You want each scene to carry consequence, or at least the *threat* of one.

Sometimes, it's about **reframing the scene** entirely. Maybe it's starting too early or ending too late. Maybe it's the wrong location. Maybe it's missing a point of view. You can ask ChatGPT, "How else could I write this scene so it begins in the middle of the conflict?" or "What's a more dynamic version of this moment that uses action instead of dialogue?" Don't be afraid to flip it on its head. Try a new format. Rewrite it backwards. Let the character lie. Let someone interrupt. You're not locked into what you wrote first.

Once you've rewritten for punch, *test it*. Read it aloud. Run it through ChatGPT again and ask, "Is this scene more impactful now?" or "Where could I dial up the emotional intensity even more?" Keep shaping, refining, and playing until it crackles.

Because a punchy scene doesn't just sit there—it *moves*. It hits. It shifts something. The best scenes don't just tell the story—they *are* the story. And rewriting with punch is about pulling the most out of every beat, every line, and every moment.

With ChatGPT as your tag-team partner, there's no reason to settle for scenes that just do the job. You can aim higher. You can write scenes that knock the wind out of people. That leave a mark.

Because when every scene punches above its weight, your pilot doesn't just get read—it gets remembered.

Using ChatGPT to Develop Episode Titles and Themes

One of the most enjoyable parts of shaping a TV series is coming up with episode titles and the themes that thread through each one. Titles are tiny storytelling opportunities. Themes are emotional and philosophical blueprints. Together, they set the tone, suggest meaning, and create curiosity. In a well-written series, each episode feels like its own short story—anchored by a core idea and wrapped in a name that hints at what lies inside. Whether you're going for clever, cryptic, poetic, or punchy, the process of finding titles and themes becomes a lot easier—and a lot more fun—with ChatGPT by your side.

Let's start with titles. A good episode title does more than just label—it teases. It provokes thought. It draws a line between narrative and meaning. Some series go minimalist (*Lost, Barry, Severance*). Others lean into literary flair (*Grey's Anatomy*, *BoJack Horseman*, *Breaking Bad*). Some are humorous, some mysterious, and some reveal themselves only after the episode ends. No matter your style, ChatGPT can be used like a creative boardroom of brainstorming minds working in real time.

All you have to do is give a little direction. For example, you can say:

"Give me ten episode titles for a series about a con artist pretending to be a therapist," or

"Suggest poetic episode titles for a dystopian sci-fi show about memory manipulation."

ChatGPT will return a list that ranges in tone, structure, and reference—some elegant, some edgy. You might keep one exactly as-is, or combine two to form your own. It's the quickest way to break out of the same-old title rut and explore fresh territory.

Maybe you have a specific episode in mind, but you don't yet know what to call it. That's another perfect use case. You can describe the plot and ask, "What's a fitting episode title that captures the emotional arc of this story?" ChatGPT will help translate plot into metaphor, wordplay, irony, or tone—whatever best suits your series voice.

And if you have a series where each episode title follows a particular convention—say, all are one-word titles, or all reference song lyrics, or all are thematic riddles—you can let ChatGPT know. For example: "Generate titles for a crime series where every episode is named after a tarot card," or "Give me ten pun-based titles for a comedy about roommates running a failing food truck." The AI quickly adapts and keeps things on-brand across the entire season.

Themes, on the other hand, are about *emotional architecture*. Every episode, no matter how plot-heavy, should be saying something beneath the surface. What's the emotional or moral question at the heart of the story? What is each character struggling with? How do the subplots echo or contrast the main theme? You don't always need to state it out loud—but as the writer, you should know what it is. And with ChatGPT, you can mine your stories for their thematic undercurrent.

Start by asking: "What's the central emotional theme of this episode where a cop chooses between loyalty and justice?" or "Help me identify the unifying theme in this episode where a woman gets trapped in her childhood home during a storm." ChatGPT will give you phrases like *betrayal vs. duty*, *fear of change*, *the illusion of safety*, or *what it means to grow up*. These phrases help you design character arcs, emotional reversals, and even scene transitions.

You can also use ChatGPT to align theme and title. Maybe your episode is about control slipping away. Ask, "What's a poetic title that reflects the theme of losing control?" You might get options like *The Thread*, *Off the Rails*, or *Unraveled*. These options now help define not just the title, but the lens through which you shape scenes and dialogue.

Another approach is to give ChatGPT a list of your episode loglines and say, "Assign a theme and a title to each of these episodes." In minutes, you've got a framework for your entire season. Each title reflects tone, and each theme becomes a guide for character development and story rhythm.

And it's not just for drama. For comedies, ChatGPT can be a goldmine of cleverness. Ask it to "Generate Friends-style episode titles where every episode starts with 'The One Where...'" or "Write ironic titles for a workplace comedy about disaster recovery agents." If your show leans genre, you can request horror-themed, noir-flavoured, or anime-inspired titles. ChatGPT adjusts instantly, and keeps ideas flowing no matter how weird or niche your concept gets.

Sometimes it helps to develop theme and title at the same time. Say you've got a basic plot: your protagonist finds out a friend betrayed them, but then learns the betrayal was meant to protect them. You might say, "Suggest a theme for this story and a title that plays off it," and get something like: *The Cost of Protection*, theme: *sacrifice disguised as betrayal*. That one-two punch gives your episode shape and emotional clarity.

Titles and themes also help you track balance in your season. Maybe you realize five episodes are all themed around loss, and none explore hope or identity. That's when you can say, "Give me themes that contrast with the ones I already have," and ChatGPT helps you expand your emotional range. You can even ask it to arrange the titles to form a subtle narrative pattern across the season, or show escalation.

If you're working on a show bible or pitch deck, this becomes especially useful. A great set of episode titles and themes not only makes your season feel well thought-out—it makes it *exciting*. It tells producers, agents, or execs that you're not winging it. You know where the story's going, what it's saying, and how every piece fits.

Ultimately, titles and themes aren't just labels and ideas. They're invitations. A title invites us to watch. A theme invites us to feel. And with ChatGPT, you're never stuck staring at a blank page trying to come up with something clever or meaningful. You're building a season where every episode speaks, and every name carries weight.

Because in TV, episodes come and go. But the right title, wrapped around the right idea? That sticks. That lingers. That makes people want to see what you'll say next.

How to Brainstorm B-Stories with ChatGPT

In television writing, the A-story does the heavy lifting—it's the main plot, the driver of tension, the heart of the episode. But the B-story? That's where your show starts to breathe. The B-story gives depth to side characters, adds emotional texture, provides comic relief or contrast, and sometimes even delivers the most memorable moments of the episode. Done right, the B-story supports or subtly reflects the A-story in theme or tone. Done poorly, it feels like filler. The trick is crafting a B-story that feels intentional, connected, and entertaining—and with ChatGPT, brainstorming them becomes not just easy but wildly creative.

The first place to start is with the purpose of your B-story. Is it there to deepen a relationship? Introduce a subplot that will expand later in the season? Offer thematic contrast? Or just let the audience catch their breath between high-stakes scenes? Knowing this helps you shape the tone and structure of the subplot. You can ask ChatGPT directly: "What's a B-story idea that contrasts with a dramatic A-story about betrayal?" or "Give me a subplot that mirrors the theme of control and surrender." Instantly, you get suggestions that are not just random ideas, but specifically tuned to echo or balance your main plot.

Sometimes you're starting with characters, not plot. Maybe you have a supporting character you love, and you want to give them a moment to shine. You can ask ChatGPT, "What's a funny or emotional subplot for a character who's usually the comic relief but needs more depth?" or "Give me a romantic misadventure for the protagonist's best friend that runs alongside the main investigation." This kind of character-first brainstorming is a great way to flesh out your ensemble while still anchoring each episode in emotional and thematic cohesion.

If your A-story is heavy on action or suspense, your B-story might be smaller, more personal. If your A-story is quiet and emotional, your B-story might be where you add levity or absurdity. The two stories don't have to be the same—but they should *talk to each other*. ChatGPT is fantastic at helping you link them. Try: "Suggest a B-story that thematically parallels a main plot about forgiveness," and it might give you a subplot where another character tries to forgive themselves for something unrelated—but emotionally resonant.

You can also build B-stories around *problems*, not just plot. Ask, "What's a conflict two side characters could have that plays out while the main story unfolds?" or "Give me a subplot where a small lie spirals out of control during a quiet episode." These types of storylines are often goldmines for character development and can easily tie back into the tone or theme of the A-story.

Don't forget that B-stories can advance long-term arcs too. Maybe your A-story is self-contained, but the B-story starts to sow seeds for a future twist, relationship, or reveal. Ask ChatGPT, "What's a subtle subplot I can introduce here that sets up a big event in episode five?" or "How can I use this B-story to hint at a character's hidden agenda?" This is how you build narrative momentum and audience investment over time.

You can even structure your B-story brainstorming like a writer's room session. Tell ChatGPT, "We're breaking episode four of a sci-fi series. The A-story is about the crew surviving a planet storm. Brainstorm three B-story options involving secondary characters." You'll get ideas tailored to your existing plot and characters. You can then riff off those suggestions, expand, or combine them into something uniquely yours.

It's also useful to test the pacing and placement of your B-story within the episode. Ask, "Where should I introduce the B-story for best narrative rhythm?" or "How can I resolve the B-plot so it echoes the ending of the A-plot?" This helps avoid common pitfalls like awkward transitions or storylines that fizzle out instead of landing with purpose.

Let's say your A-story is about a high-stakes legal battle. A great B-story might be something much smaller—maybe one of the junior associates is trying to sneak out for a date without their boss noticing. Funny, right? But now ask ChatGPT, "How can this B-story subtly reflect the theme of truth versus deception?" Suddenly, it's not just a throwaway—it's connected. The stakes are smaller, but the emotional energy is linked. That's how you give your episode depth without distracting from the main narrative.

You can also reverse engineer it. Say you already have a great B-story idea. You can ask ChatGPT, "What kind of A-story would contrast well with this subplot about a character trying to win back their cat from an ex?" or "What tone should the A-plot carry if this B-plot is emotionally heavy?" The AI becomes your sounding board for tone balancing and structural flow.

Another fun use: give ChatGPT a list of episode A-stories from your season and ask it to suggest unique B-stories for each one that don't feel repetitive. It'll keep your subplots fresh, diverse, and on-theme. You can even ask, "What's a seasonal B-story arc I can build across all ten episodes for a side character?" and develop mini character journeys that reward long-term viewers.

And when you're stuck? Just say, "I need a B-plot. Anything. Weird, funny, emotional, small. Let's go." Let ChatGPT throw ideas at the wall. You might find one that makes you laugh, or one that surprises you. B-stories are playgrounds—you can afford to be loose and creative with them. They don't carry the show's weight, but they can be where the show *wins hearts.*

Because at the end of the day, a strong B-story makes your world feel lived-in, your characters more human, and your episode richer. And with ChatGPT helping you generate, shape, and refine those side journeys, you don't have to settle for "something on the side." You can write subplots that sing.

And when your A-story drives the episode while the B-story lifts it emotionally or thematically? That's when your show truly starts to soar.

Developing Antagonists That Aren't Just Villains

When we think of antagonists, our minds often go straight to villains—cold, calculating, morally bankrupt people out to destroy the hero. But in the world of television, especially in pilot writing, antagonists can and *should* be much more complex than that. The most compelling antagonists aren't mustache-twirling bad guys. They're often people who genuinely believe they're right, people who challenge the protagonist's values, people whose presence *forces* the hero to change. The real power of an antagonist isn't in how evil they are—it's in how deeply they push against the main character's arc. And with ChatGPT as your brainstorming partner, you can develop layered, unpredictable, and emotionally rich antagonists who elevate your pilot from good to unforgettable.

Let's start with the simplest truth: an antagonist is anyone who stands in the way of what your protagonist wants. That's it. They don't have to be cruel, violent, or even wrong. They just have to create resistance. That resistance can come from a rival, a parent, a friend, a system, or even a belief. You can ask ChatGPT, "Who or what could stand in the way of my protagonist achieving their goal in this episode?" and you'll get a range of possibilities, many of which aren't traditional villains at all.

The best antagonists believe they're the *hero* of their own story. They're not trying to be difficult—they're trying to do what *they* think is right. ChatGPT can help you shape this by asking, "What does this antagonist believe in so deeply that it puts them in direct conflict with the protagonist?" or "How can I make this character's motives feel justified, even noble?" Suddenly, your antagonist isn't just an obstacle—they're a reflection of an opposing worldview.

This dynamic is especially rich when the antagonist and protagonist want the *same thing*, but go about it in completely different ways. Maybe they both want justice, but one follows the law and the other bends it. Maybe they both want love, but one hides emotion and the other demands honesty. These kinds of antagonists create emotional and philosophical tension. Ask ChatGPT, "Give me an antagonist who mirrors the hero's goals but has a fundamentally different approach," and you'll get ideas that create complex, layered conflict.

Another powerful technique is building antagonists out of *relationships*. A parent who wants to protect their child, even if it means stifling their dreams. A boss who thinks they're mentoring someone, while actually holding them back. These aren't villains—they're people with their own goals and fears, and that's what makes the conflict more real. Try prompting ChatGPT with, "Suggest a relationship-based antagonist who believes they're helping the protagonist," and it'll offer characters that feel emotionally grounded and painfully human.

You can also explore *ideological antagonism*. Maybe your protagonist believes in freedom, and the antagonist believes in order. Or your protagonist is fueled by hope, and the antagonist believes hope is dangerous. These aren't just personal differences—they're thematic engines that drive the entire series. ChatGPT can help here too: "What belief system could this antagonist hold that clashes with my protagonist's arc of learning to trust?" This not only builds tension but makes every scene between them feel purposeful and meaningful.

Sometimes the best antagonists are the ones who *used to be allies*. Think about how many great shows thrive on the slow burn of a partnership breaking down. Best friends become rivals. Mentors become enemies. Lovers become strangers. That slow shift from alignment to opposition gives your story emotional weight. Ask ChatGPT, "What's a reason this former ally could become an antagonist without turning evil?" or "How can I show the cracks in this friendship before it collapses?" and you'll start layering subtext and tension before anything explodes.

Even when your antagonist *is* a more traditional villain, they don't have to be one-note. Give them a personal code. Give them something or someone they love. Give them vulnerability. ChatGPT is great at this. You can say, "What's a contradiction in this antagonist's personality that makes them more human?" or "What's a quiet moment that shows this character's inner conflict?" Suddenly, they're not just there to create chaos—they're a character we can understand, maybe even sympathize with.

Another angle is to create *situational antagonists*. These are characters who aren't "bad" at all—they just have goals that conflict with the protagonist's in this specific moment. A new boss. A rival applicant. A by-the-book cop. The antagonist might even switch roles by the next episode, depending on the story. Ask ChatGPT, "Give me a temporary antagonist for this pilot episode who challenges the hero but could become an ally later," and you'll build scenes full of shifting dynamics and dramatic tension.

Antagonists can also represent *internal conflict*. Sometimes, your character is their own worst enemy—but that inner struggle can be externalized through another character. Someone who triggers their insecurities. Someone who represents the path they fear. Ask ChatGPT, "How can I externalize my protagonist's fear of failure through a rival character?" and you'll start writing scenes where the conflict feels both personal and symbolic.

The antagonist's role in your pilot is to create pressure. Pressure reveals who the protagonist really is. Under pressure, people crack, reveal truths, make terrible choices, or show surprising strength. A good antagonist doesn't just block the hero—they *test* them. They force the hero to grow—or double down on a flaw. With ChatGPT, you can ask, "How can this antagonist force my protagonist to make a morally gray decision in the pilot?" and you'll get story fuel that drives both plot and character.

Ultimately, the goal is to make your antagonist feel *inevitable*. Like the story wouldn't work without them. And that happens when you build them not as a foil, but as a force. Someone who brings out the worst—and sometimes the best—in your protagonist.

With ChatGPT helping you explore their psychology, backstory, contradictions, and motivations, you can create antagonists who are just as compelling—maybe even more compelling—than your lead.

Because in a great series, the antagonist isn't just an obstacle. They're the reason we *have* a story.

Setting Up the Unexpected for Episode Two

The final moments of your pilot aren't just about wrapping up the story—they're about cracking it open. A great pilot gives the audience something satisfying, but it also leaves them with a burning question or a sudden twist that makes them desperate for episode two. This doesn't have to be a cliffhanger in the traditional sense. It just needs to *upend expectations*. It's the moment when the audience realizes, "Oh... this isn't the story I thought it was going to be." And that moment of surprise, that pivot or promise of deeper mystery, is one of the best things you can plan while writing your pilot. With ChatGPT, you can brainstorm twists, secrets, reversals, and surprises tailored perfectly to your story's tone and arc—so episode two doesn't just continue the story, it *elevates* it.

Let's start with the question: what would the audience *assume* by the end of your pilot? Do they think they know who the main character is? What the show is about? Where it's going? Then ask: what's a way to gently or radically flip that assumption in the last minute? ChatGPT can help you break the pattern. Try a prompt like, "Suggest three unexpected final beats for a workplace drama that seems resolved by the end of the pilot," and you'll get suggestions that open doors the audience didn't know existed.

There are several classic ways to land an unexpected hook. One is the **reveal of a hidden truth**—something the characters (or audience) didn't know that recontextualizes everything. It could be that the sidekick is actually a spy. That the whole case was a setup. That the protagonist lied to the audience. You can ask ChatGPT, "What's a twist ending that flips the emotional meaning of the pilot?" or "Reveal something about the protagonist that changes the viewer's trust in them." These last-minute revelations don't feel cheap if they've been subtly seeded throughout the episode.

Another way to shake up expectations is to **break the rules of the world**. Maybe your show seemed grounded—then suddenly you introduce a supernatural element. Or you've hinted at a normal relationship story, and then someone is revealed to be leading a double life. ChatGPT can help you calibrate tone here. You can say, "What's a twist that adds genre without breaking the realism of the pilot?" or "How do I introduce a sci-fi element at the end of a show that starts as a romance?"

Then there's the **arrival of a new threat or ally**. The pilot sets up a clear antagonist or situation, and just as that gets resolved or accepted, *boom*—something (or someone) new shows up. A body drops. A rival enters. A character presumed dead walks through the door. These moments expand the story's scope and raise fresh stakes. Ask ChatGPT, "Introduce a character in the last scene who changes the entire direction of the next episode," and it'll give you candidates that raise eyebrows and heart rates.

Sometimes the unexpected isn't about a big twist—it's about a **new question**. The protagonist gets what they want... but why doesn't it feel right? A couple kisses... but one of them looks over their shoulder with regret. The main character reaches a goal... and discovers it comes with a terrifying new responsibility. These are quieter pivots, but they still hook deeply. You can use ChatGPT to generate emotional questions like, "What's a small but powerful beat that creates an emotional dilemma for episode two?" or "How can I suggest that everything the character wanted may not be enough?"

Another powerful technique is the **delayed explanation**. You can end the pilot with a strong image or event—a decision, an arrival, a reaction—but not explain what it means until the next episode. This only works if the setup feels intentional, not confusing. Ask ChatGPT, "What's an ambiguous final image that creates anticipation for a mystery?" or "How can I end this pilot on a bold move without explaining the character's motivation yet?" Ambiguity, done right, pulls viewers straight into the next chapter.

Tone matters here too. If your show is funny, your surprise might be absurd or ironic. If it's dramatic, it might be devastating. If it's a mystery, it might be something that solves one riddle while creating another. You can even test multiple tones with ChatGPT. Ask, "Give me three versions of an unexpected final moment: one dramatic, one comedic, one surreal," and you can compare what feels most true to your series.

And let's not forget the **character turn**. One of the best ways to promise growth or conflict in episode two is to end your pilot with a character doing something you never thought they'd do. The quiet one starts shouting. The brave one backs down. The honest one lies. These moments leave the audience not just wondering what will happen next, but *who* the character will become. Ask ChatGPT, "What's a character decision that would surprise the audience but feel emotionally earned?" and it will help you plant twists that grow out of real internal conflict.

Once you land on a strong final beat, don't just drop it in—**set it up**. Layer it in with foreshadowing, tension, or even misdirection throughout the pilot. You want the audience to gasp when it happens—but also be able to look back and say, "Ohhh... that's why that happened." Ask ChatGPT, "What small clues can I plant earlier that make this twist feel inevitable in hindsight?" and it'll help you reverse-engineer the surprise into the spine of the script.

Finally, remember that the unexpected doesn't have to explode. Sometimes, it's a whisper. A glance. A door left open. A voicemail unheard. The beauty of using ChatGPT is that you can try ten different versions of that moment in ten different styles, moods, and formats—and then pick the one that doesn't just shock, but *intrigues*.

Because when the pilot ends, the viewer should feel one thing above all else:

"I need to know what happens next."

And setting up the unexpected is how you earn that feeling—one scene, one reveal, one twist at a time.

Writing the Series Bible with ChatGPT

The series bible is the backbone of your TV project. It's not just a summary—it's a blueprint, a pitch deck, and a creative manifesto rolled into one. It tells producers, executives, agents, and collaborators that you haven't just written a pilot—you've envisioned an entire world, a cast of characters who can grow for years, and story arcs that stretch far beyond the first episode. A solid series bible says: *this isn't just a script, this is a show.* And with ChatGPT, you can build that bible piece by piece, faster and smarter, while keeping your unique voice at the center of it all.

So what goes into a great series bible? There's no one fixed format, but most include the show's concept, tone, setting, character breakdowns, pilot summary, episode summaries, season arcs, themes, and stylistic notes. It can be a ten-page document or a sprawling creative dossier—but it must be clear, compelling, and consistent. And ChatGPT can help you develop each section step-by-step.

Start with your **logline**, the one-sentence hook that sells the entire show. This is your first impression. You can ask ChatGPT, "Help me write a compelling logline for a drama about a disgraced surgeon rebuilding his life in a remote town," and it'll return multiple variations—tight, punchy, and pitch-friendly. Want it funnier, darker, or more poetic? Just say the word.

Next, craft your **series overview**. This is your chance to explain what the show *is*, what it's about emotionally and narratively, and what the viewer is signing up for. You might say to ChatGPT, "Write a series overview in the tone of a prestige thriller that explores guilt, justice, and identity," and you'll get a well-structured paragraph or two that sets the tone and theme. You can then polish it or merge multiple versions.

The **tone and style** section is where you describe how the show *feels*. Is it gritty, grounded, heightened, comedic, surreal, slow-burn, or fast-paced? Is it shot like a documentary or with cinematic scope? Here, ChatGPT can help you compare your show to others without sounding derivative. Try, "Write a paragraph describing the tone of this series as a mix between *Euphoria* and *Sharp Objects*," and you'll get a vivid mood board in text form.

Then come the **character breakdowns**. These should be more than just bios—they should capture essence, motivation, contradictions, and arcs. Start with your protagonist. Ask ChatGPT, "Write a character breakdown for a reluctant cult leader who accidentally becomes a revolutionary," and you'll get a compelling snapshot of a character in conflict. Do the same for supporting characters, and be sure to include how they relate to the central theme or dynamic. You can even ask, "Suggest three flaws that could create conflict for this character," or "How might this character evolve across five seasons?"

Your **pilot summary** should be concise but vivid. Summarize the plot while capturing the emotional beats, major twists, and tone. If your pilot is already written, you can paste it in and say, "Summarize this pilot script in two paragraphs for a series bible," and ChatGPT will highlight the key beats. If it's not written yet, describe the story and ask, "Turn this into a tight summary of the pilot episode."

The **season overview** section outlines what happens beyond the pilot. Where is the story going? What is the arc of season one? Where might things head in season two and beyond? You don't need to spoil everything—you just need to show that there's enough story to sustain a full season and then some. Ask ChatGPT, "Outline a 10-episode arc for a crime drama where the detective becomes the suspect," and you'll get a skeleton you can expand or restructure to match your vision.

You can also include **episode summaries**, which are one-paragraph breakdowns of each episode in the first season. This is especially helpful for serialized shows. Ask, "Write one-paragraph summaries for each episode of a six-part political thriller," and ChatGPT can help you map out a progression of tension, escalation, twists, and payoffs.

Another important section is **themes**. What deeper questions does the show explore? Identity, power, family, survival, truth, love, redemption? You can ask ChatGPT, "Write a paragraph on how this series explores the theme of control vs. chaos," and it will help you articulate the emotional and philosophical layers of your show without getting too academic or abstract.

Don't forget **visual references**. If you're including images or a mood board, you can ask ChatGPT to write the descriptive copy: "Describe the visual style of this series as if it were pitched to Netflix, referencing tone, lighting, and camera movement." You'll get studio-ready language that helps communicate your creative vision.

And finally, include your **series engine**—what drives the show from episode to episode? Is it a case-of-the-week format? A long-running mystery? An emotional journey with evolving character dynamics? Ask ChatGPT, "Explain the storytelling engine of a time-loop series that reveals new truths each episode," and you'll get something concise and intelligent that reads like you've been pitching this show for years.

Once you have all these pieces, ChatGPT can help you **organize and polish the document**. Say, "Help me structure my series bible into a clean, flowing format with section headers," and it'll turn your raw content into a presentable, professional outline. You can even ask for help naming sections with style, like "Title suggestions for character breakdowns that match a noir vibe."

Writing a series bible can feel overwhelming, especially when you're doing everything else too—drafting scripts, developing characters, world-building, planning future seasons. But with ChatGPT, you don't have to do it all from scratch or alone. You can brainstorm, edit, experiment, and refine every element until the whole thing reads like a confident, cohesive, exciting vision.

Because at the end of the day, your series bible isn't just a document. It's a promise. A pitch. A plan. It tells the industry, the audience, and yourself:

This is a world worth building. And I know exactly how to build it.

Creating a Pitch Deck from the Pilot Script

A pitch deck is your visual handshake. It's the sleek, curated presentation that introduces your series to producers, networks, agents, and collaborators. It's not a full script—it's the *invitation* to read the script. While your pilot does the storytelling, the pitch deck shows the big picture: the world, the tone, the characters, the themes, and why this show matters now. It's both creative and strategic. And the good news is, once your pilot is written, the pitch deck practically builds itself—with a little help from ChatGPT guiding you through the layout, wording, and polish.

Think of your pitch deck as a beautiful, bite-sized version of your series bible—but faster, lighter, and more focused on selling the *vibe*. A good pitch deck should be visual, emotionally engaging, and easy to skim. You don't want to overwhelm people with information. You want them to *feel* like they already know your show after flipping through a few pages. With ChatGPT, you can quickly turn your pilot content into each of the major pitch deck sections, styled in whatever tone or format you need.

Start with the **Title Page**. This is your show's name, a logline, and optionally a subtitle or tagline that hints at the tone. Ask ChatGPT, "Write a tagline for a sci-fi series about memory theft," and it'll deliver options ranging from poetic to punchy. You can test variations: bold, mysterious, funny—whatever best reflects your brand.

Next is the **Series Overview** page. This is a paragraph or two that captures the core premise of your show. What's the hook? What's it really about? You're not telling the whole story—you're setting up the problem, the protagonist, and the world. Say to ChatGPT, "Write a series overview based on this pilot script about a washed-up journalist uncovering a government cover-up," and it'll give you copy that feels professional and intriguing.

Then comes the **Tone & Style** page. This is your visual identity statement. What does the show *feel* like? What is the viewer's emotional experience supposed to be? You can describe this directly or through comparisons—"*Succession* meets *Black Mirror* with a hint of *Mad Men*." Ask ChatGPT, "Help me write a tone and style paragraph for a darkly comedic workplace thriller," and it will describe mood, pacing, lighting, music, and atmosphere in a tight, studio-friendly paragraph.

Your **Character Pages** are next. Highlight the key players—your protagonist, antagonist, and the essential supporting cast. Include one paragraph per character describing their personality, their role in the story, and their personal arc. Don't just list traits—talk about desires, conflicts, contradictions. ChatGPT can help here too. Paste in your character notes or pilot scenes and say, "Summarize this character for a pitch deck," and it'll return a polished paragraph that reads clean, compelling, and layered.

Some decks include a **World/Setting** page. This is where you describe where the show takes place. If your story is grounded in reality, this could be a specific town, subculture, or professional world. If it's genre—sci-fi, fantasy, dystopia—you need to set the rules clearly. Ask ChatGPT, "Write a one-paragraph description of a near-future city controlled by corporate surveillance," and it'll give you something poetic or practical, depending on your request.

Then there's the **Pilot Synopsis** page. This is a short, structured summary of the pilot episode—start to finish, hitting the big beats. No scene-by-scene breakdown, just the flow of major events and emotional turns. If your pilot is finished, you can even paste it in and ask ChatGPT, "Write a one-paragraph summary of this script for a pitch deck," and you'll get a version that makes the episode feel engaging and complete without giving too much away.

Now you want to talk about the **Season Arc**. What happens after the pilot? Where does the show go? You don't have to map every beat, but you should sketch the journey—what your protagonist is facing, what new layers will unfold, and where the story is ultimately headed. Ask ChatGPT, "Give me a season one arc for this political thriller pilot where the protagonist becomes the villain," and it'll lay out a tension-building roadmap you can refine.

Many decks include **Episode Samples** or **Episode Ideas**—short blurbs for 4–8 future episodes that show the range of your series. These should reflect tone, variety, and long-term potential. You can brainstorm with ChatGPT by saying, "Give me 6 episode ideas for a romantic dramedy about two exes who become business partners," and it'll generate a list you can edit or expand.

A good pitch deck also includes a **Themes Page**. This is where you reflect on what the show is really about beneath the surface. Love, identity, betrayal, healing, power, justice—whatever's at the heart of your story. Ask ChatGPT, "Write a short paragraph on how this series explores the theme of redemption," and you'll get something that's meaningful but not too heavy-handed.

Finally, some decks end with a **Why Now?** or **Closing Statement** page. This is your chance to speak from the heart and say why this show matters—why it's timely, personal, or necessary. This section can be earnest, emotional, or culturally reflective. Ask ChatGPT, "Help me write a closing statement for a series about climate disaster and human survival," and it'll help you put your passion into words.

As you assemble all of these sections, ChatGPT can also help you rewrite, polish, and format. Ask, "Rewrite this in a more stylish, HBO-style tone," or "Make this language more network-friendly," or "Give this pitch more urgency and clarity." It's like having a tone editor at your fingertips.

Visually, your pitch deck should feel like your show. Use reference images, concept art, stills, or even AI-generated visuals to give it a cinematic feel. If you're including images, you can ask ChatGPT to write the captions or even suggest what kinds of visuals would best match the tone: "What kind of imagery fits a neo-noir detective show set in a digital surveillance state?"

And once it's done? Ask ChatGPT to help you test it. Say, "Read this pitch deck like a studio exec. What questions would you have?" or "What's missing from this pitch deck if I want to present to Netflix?" You'll get a feedback loop that makes sure you're not missing key elements before the real pitch.

A great pitch deck is a calling card, a mood board, and a promise. With your pilot script as the foundation and ChatGPT helping you craft every section with clarity, creativity, and style, you'll walk into any room—physical or virtual—knowing your show isn't just on paper.

Testing the Market with a One-Day Written Pilot

So you've just written a pilot script in a single day with ChatGPT—a full episode from concept to final scene, fast, focused, and thrilling. You're proud of it, excited by it, maybe even a little surprised by how well it flows. But now comes the next question: *Is this marketable?* Writing a pilot in one day is a bold and creative achievement, but the real magic happens when you start testing that pilot out in the real world—seeing how it lands, how people respond, and what it tells you about the market you're writing for. With the right tools, strategy, and ChatGPT as your co-pilot, you can take that script from zero to test-ready and see whether you've struck gold or found something that needs another layer of polish.

Testing the market doesn't mean throwing it out on social media and hoping someone bites. It means gathering informed reactions, simulating industry feedback, and figuring out what audience, buyer, or platform your show might connect with. And the beauty of using ChatGPT is that you don't need to wait for a producer to validate your work—you can run simulations, craft materials, and even roleplay meetings before you send it to a single human being.

Start by identifying your **audience segment**. Who is this pilot *for*? Is it aimed at young adults, prestige-drama lovers, sci-fi fans, horror junkies, network comedy viewers? If you're not sure, ChatGPT can help you pinpoint this. Ask, "Based on this pilot script, what audience would be most drawn to this show?" or "What age group and platform is best suited for this kind of story?" You'll get a target audience breakdown that instantly clarifies how to position the show.

Once you know your audience, ask ChatGPT to generate **test-reader personas**. For example, say, "Pretend you're a 24-year-old Netflix development assistant reading this pilot—what's your reaction?" or "As an Amazon Studios exec looking for a mystery series, does this concept fit your slate?" ChatGPT will respond in-character, pointing out what works, what might not, and where the story aligns with platform trends. You can run this test over and over, changing personas, ages, networks, and tastes. It's like having your own private panel of readers.

You can also create **mini focus group tests**. Give ChatGPT a short description of your pilot and ask, "What questions would an audience have after watching this episode?" or "What elements of this story might make viewers tune in—or tune out?" This gives you a sense of what's clear, what's confusing, and where the emotional hooks are. If you're unsure how the cold open lands or whether your cliffhanger feels strong enough, ChatGPT can offer a fast pulse check before you start making revisions.

Another powerful tool is generating **market comps**—comparable shows that yours is similar to in theme, tone, or structure. Ask, "What current or recent shows are similar in tone and audience to this pilot?" or "What series could I reference when pitching this to Netflix or Hulu?" These comps are crucial for pitching and positioning, and knowing how your show fits into (or stands apart from) market trends makes a huge difference when you're trying to get it seen.

If you're thinking about **taking your pilot public**, say on a script competition website, a screenwriter forum, or a feedback group, use ChatGPT to prepare a summary, logline, and cover note that speaks directly to the intended reader. You can ask, "Write a short, confident cover letter for a one-hour thriller pilot I'm submitting to a screenwriting contest," and you'll get a tight, compelling intro that frames your one-day script as the high-concept project it is—not just something written quickly, but something written with clarity and purpose.

Now let's talk **platform matching**. Different networks and streamers have very different needs. ABC wants something different than A24. Apple TV+ might lean prestige and glossy, while FX wants edge and character. ChatGPT can help you match your pilot to buyers by saying, "Based on this pilot, which streaming platform or network would be the best fit?" or "Which production companies are likely to be interested in dark comedies about dysfunctional families?" This lets you start building a pitch strategy before you've even typed a query email.

One of the most useful features of ChatGPT is the ability to **simulate pitch meetings**. Try this: "Act as a skeptical exec. I'm going to pitch my show to you—ask me tough questions." Then respond in character. You'll get grilled about originality, audience, themes, episode count, castability, and more. It's fun, informative, and prepares you for the real thing. You can also reverse it—have ChatGPT pitch *your* show back to you. If it stumbles, that tells you the core idea might need tightening.

For real-world feedback, once you've refined your pilot and summary, consider testing it in **online screenwriting communities**, but do so smartly. Use ChatGPT to write a short blurb that invites feedback without oversharing. For example, say, "Write a short post asking for feedback on a serialized dramedy pilot about adult siblings inheriting a cult." It will help you sound professional and hook potential readers who might become collaborators, critics, or fans.

Finally, think about **next steps**. If the market test goes well—if your script lands, excites, and generates strong simulated or real feedback—use ChatGPT to draft your next materials: a pitch deck, a query letter, or a follow-up episode outline. If the response is mixed, use it to identify what to revise. Ask, "What scenes in this pilot could be hurting its market appeal?" or "What feedback should I prioritize in the next draft?"

Just remember—writing a pilot in one day doesn't mean it's rushed. It means it's *focused*. It's born from creative momentum, not hesitation. With a clear concept, clean execution, and ChatGPT as your creative partner, you're testing the market with something fresh, fast, and full of potential.

Because in today's screenwriting world, speed isn't the enemy of quality. It's the starting point. And if your one-day pilot can make people feel, think, and want more? Then you've already won the first round.

Taking Your Pilot from First Draft to First Production

You've written your pilot. Maybe you did it in a single day with ChatGPT, riding the high of creative momentum and finishing with a script that actually *works*. It has structure, character, tone, dialogue—everything you need to tell a compelling first story in a bigger world. But the end of the first draft isn't the end of the road—it's the start of the real journey. Taking your pilot from that early version to a finished production means stepping into a new mindset. You're no longer just the writer. You're the showrunner in training, the creative producer, the pitch artist, the visionary who now has to shepherd this story from paper to screen. And that's where things get exciting—and where ChatGPT can keep helping, every step of the way.

The first thing to do is assess your draft with fresh eyes. This is not about tearing it apart—it's about reading it like a director, a producer, a cast member. You can use ChatGPT to simulate that. Say, "Read this pilot as if you're a director considering shooting it—what are your biggest concerns?" Or, "What production challenges does this script present on a low budget?" You'll get practical feedback—not just about story or pacing, but about logistics, location use, cast size, and production flow.

From there, start shaping your **rewrite phase** with production in mind. Are there scenes that can be simplified? Combined? Are there locations that feel expensive or too scattered for a tight shoot? Ask ChatGPT, "What scenes in this script could be consolidated to make it more shootable?" or "Suggest ways to rewrite this set-piece scene for a smaller location with fewer characters." These are the kind of changes that keep your vision strong while making it actually filmable.

Now that you're rewriting with production in mind, think about your **shooting script** format. If your pilot was written casually or with stylistic freedom, now's the time to convert it into industry-standard formatting, ready for actors, crew, and scheduling. ChatGPT can assist with that too. Ask, "Help me format this scene for a professional shooting script," and it'll guide you on standard action line formatting, character cues, dialogue spacing, and scene headings.

Once your script is ready for eyes beyond your own, prepare a **production-ready pitch**. That means not only refining your pitch deck and series bible, but writing loglines, blurbs, and visual synopses that can be shared with cinematographers, producers, or potential collaborators. Ask ChatGPT, "Write a short pitch I can send to a filmmaker interested in directing this pilot," and it'll give you concise, engaging language that makes your project easy to understand and easy to love.

Then it's time to think about **assembling your team**. If you're producing independently, you'll need a director, a small crew, a cast, and someone handling logistics. You can use ChatGPT to write your outreach messages. Try, "Write a friendly email to a local director I admire, asking if they'd consider reading my pilot script for potential collaboration." You can even create job listings: "Write a short casting call for a lead female role, age 30s, emotionally complex, former journalist," and you'll have professional material ready to post.

Planning the actual production starts with breaking the script into parts. You'll need **scene breakdowns**, **location lists**, **prop needs**, and **character appearances by scene**. You can give ChatGPT your script and ask, "Break this script down by scene with locations and characters listed," and it will build a production breakdown you can use for your shoot schedule. You can also say, "List all props mentioned or implied in this script," and it will help you begin the pre-production checklist.

If you're working with a small or no budget, ChatGPT can help you **adapt the project to your resources**. Ask, "How can I shoot this pilot with minimal locations and a crew of five?" or "Suggest a rewrite of this scene that eliminates the need for extras or complex sets." These constraints often unlock creativity you wouldn't have otherwise explored.

As you begin planning your shoot, you'll also need **shot lists** and **storyboards**. While ChatGPT can't draw (yet), it can help you map out a visual plan: "Describe a shot-by-shot breakdown of this scene in the style of a tense thriller," and it will generate a visual script you can use as a reference. You can even describe camera angles, lighting moods, and transitions if you're working with a cinematographer or DP.

Throughout the process, you'll be coordinating with collaborators. That means writing schedules, summaries, and plans. Ask ChatGPT, "Write a one-page production overview I can share with my cast and crew," or "Create a sample shooting schedule for a 12-page pilot script over three days." The organizational side of production is heavy—but AI can help keep the paperwork, planning, and prep from slowing you down.

Don't forget **promotion**. As you move into production, you'll want to start documenting the journey and getting people curious about your project. Ask ChatGPT, "Write a social media post announcing that I'm filming my pilot next month," or "Write a logline and hashtag combo for an indie series about AI and grief." Get people excited early—it builds momentum.

Once you're filming, stay flexible. Pilots often evolve during production. Scenes get cut. Actors improvise. The weather changes. ChatGPT can be a creative safety net even during the shoot. If you lose a location or a character drops out, ask, "How can I rewrite this scene to take place in a park with two fewer characters?" and you'll get solutions in seconds. It's like having a script doctor on standby at all times.

After the shoot, during **post-production**, ChatGPT can help you write a first cut summary for potential investors, festivals, or collaborators. "Write a one-paragraph summary of my pilot after we've finished principal photography," or "Write a professional blurb for a screener link." And when the final cut is done? Ask it to help you write emails, submission statements, or press materials.

Because taking your pilot from first draft to first production is a huge leap—but it's also the natural next step. The tools are in your hands, and with ChatGPT on your creative team, you never have to do it alone.

You've already written the story. Now it's time to *show* the world what it looks like.

Examples of ChatGPT Prompts for Pilot Idea Generation

Coming up with a fresh, compelling idea for a television pilot can sometimes feel like the hardest part of the process. Maybe you've got a vague image or a feeling you want to explore, or maybe you're completely blank, staring at the cursor waiting for inspiration to strike. The great thing about using ChatGPT is that you don't need to wait—you can prompt your way into an idea. The right prompt can unlock dozens of possibilities in seconds, and with a little curiosity and experimentation, you can generate pilot concepts that are bold, original, and market-ready. The secret is knowing *how* to ask—and that's what this chapter is about.

Let's start with the most basic prompt you can use to warm up your creativity:

"Give me five original ideas for a TV pilot."

It's broad, open-ended, and great for getting your brain moving. You'll get a mix of genres and tones—maybe a family drama, a sci-fi mystery, a workplace comedy, and something totally unexpected. From there, you can narrow your focus. Try:

"Give me five original ideas for a supernatural teen drama TV pilot."

or

"I want pilot ideas set in a small town with a dark secret."

or

"Generate a pilot idea for a single-location thriller."

These kinds of genre or setting-specific prompts help guide ChatGPT's creativity in the direction you're already leaning, while still surprising you with things you might not have thought of.

Another powerful approach is to start with a **theme** and let the concept build around it. Try prompts like:

"Give me TV pilot ideas that explore the theme of identity."

"What's a good pilot idea that examines guilt and redemption?"

"Suggest a pilot idea about betrayal, set in the music industry."

You can even ask for a certain *tone* or *style* with your theme:

"Give me a darkly comic pilot idea about loneliness."

"Write a light-hearted mystery pilot idea centered on the theme of reinvention."

Characters can also be your entry point. Try asking:

"Give me a TV pilot idea about a jaded detective who has to work with an idealistic rookie."

"Suggest a pilot idea for a show led by a morally gray female protagonist in her 40s."

"Give me five pilot ideas that feature unlikely friendships."

You can also base your prompts around **story engines**—the recurring narrative structure that drives the series. Try something like:

"Suggest a pilot idea for a weekly case-of-the-week structure that slowly reveals a larger mystery."

"Give me a concept for an anthology show where each episode revolves around a lie."

"Create a pilot concept for a serialized drama where each episode takes place in a different year."

Maybe you want to build your concept *backwards*—from the twist or ending. Ask:

"Give me a pilot idea where the final scene reveals the protagonist is the villain."

"Suggest a pilot idea where the audience realizes the narrator is unreliable at the very end."

Or maybe you want to build a concept around a **location**, which is a fantastic way to anchor your pilot in a unique, cinematic space. Prompts like:

"Give me a TV pilot idea set entirely on a cruise ship."

"What's a compelling pilot idea set in an airport?"

"Generate a drama pilot set in an underground survival bunker."

For shows with a **high concept**, you can prompt ChatGPT to combine ideas and elements:

"Give me a pilot concept that combines time travel with high school politics."

"What's a show idea that mixes courtroom drama with paranormal investigation?"

"Suggest a pilot idea that blends historical fiction with alternate reality."

You can also model your prompts after existing shows by tone, format, or genre, without copying their plots:

"Give me a pilot idea in the tone of *Succession* but set in a restaurant empire."

"Create a show like *Stranger Things* but set in a futuristic desert colony."

"Suggest a pilot idea that feels like *Fleabag* crossed with *Breaking Bad*."

If you're stuck between two ideas and can't decide which way to go, you can even say:

"I have two ideas—one about a washed-up magician solving crimes, and one about a reality show gone wrong. Help me combine these into a single, coherent pilot concept."

Once you have a rough idea, refine it. Ask:

"Expand this pilot idea into a full paragraph."

"Give me three possible episode one arcs for this concept."

"What could be the twist at the end of the pilot?"

"List five possible titles for this pilot idea."

And when you're ready to build out the world and characters:

"Describe the protagonist in more detail."

"Suggest a supporting cast for this pilot."

"What are three long-term story arcs for this series?"

Even if you don't use every idea exactly as written, these prompts kickstart your creative thinking. They help you explore unexpected angles and avoid cliché. They give you options, variations, and paths to consider—all in minutes.

The real key is staying playful. Prompting is like creative tennis: you serve, ChatGPT returns, and you keep hitting ideas back and forth until something lands that feels alive. And once you find that spark? You're not staring at a blank page anymore. You've got a pilot in the making.

Examples of ChatGPT Prompts for Story and Episode Ideas

Once you've locked in your series concept and pilot, the next challenge is figuring out what happens next. Whether you're writing a serialized drama, a comedy-of-the-week, or an anthology with fresh characters every episode, you'll need a constant flow of ideas to keep your show compelling and unpredictable. Coming up with full season arcs can be overwhelming—but if you break it down episode by episode, story by story, and prompt by prompt, you'll never run out of material. That's where ChatGPT becomes your private writer's room, ready to bounce ideas, pitch twists, and sketch out full episodes on demand.

The trick is knowing how to frame your questions to get specific, creative, and useful results. Let's start with some simple, open-ended prompts you can use to get the wheels turning:

"Give me five episode ideas for a drama series about a high-powered divorce attorney hiding a criminal past."

"Suggest ten storylines for a sci-fi show where each episode explores a different memory-altering technology."

"What are some standalone mystery episode ideas for a cozy detective series set in a small beach town?"

If you're writing a serialized show, you can start with a season concept and ask for a breakdown:

"Plot out ten escalating episodes of a conspiracy thriller where a journalist uncovers a shadow government."

"Create an episode-by-episode outline for season one of a fantasy series about a rogue witch trying to protect her village."

You can also focus on character journeys:

"Give me five episode ideas that each test a different flaw in my protagonist's personality."

"Suggest subplots that could evolve my protagonist's relationship with their estranged sibling."

"What's a storyline where the sidekick takes center stage and faces a moral choice?"

Genre-specific prompts help shape tone and expectations. Try:

"Write three story ideas for a horror series where each episode focuses on a different cursed object."

"Give me romantic comedy episode ideas involving mistaken identity and awkward reunions."

"Suggest storylines for an animated comedy about office workers in a company run by aliens."

For high-concept shows, combine opposites to create tension:

"What's a dramatic episode idea for a sci-fi series that takes place entirely during a wedding?"

"Suggest a comedic storyline in a post-apocalyptic survival show."

"Give me an episode idea that blends political satire with supernatural horror."

You can also use thematic prompts to guide deeper meaning in your stories:

"What's a storyline that explores the theme of justice versus revenge in episode three?"

"Give me an episode idea that challenges my protagonist's belief in loyalty."

"Suggest a story where every character is forced to confront a lie they've been living with."

Looking to create emotional arcs within an episode? Try:

"Plot an episode where the protagonist starts off cocky and ends humbled."

"Write an episode outline where two enemies are forced to work together and learn something about each other."

"Suggest a story that builds to a bittersweet ending that changes the course of the season."

For shows with a case-of-the-week or problem-of-the-week structure, use prompts like:

"What's a medical case that emotionally parallels the doctor's personal life?"

"Suggest a legal case for a courtroom drama that tests the firm's moral boundaries."

"Give me a weekly challenge for a reality competition series about artists that involves emotional storytelling."

If you're writing anthology-style episodes with different characters and stories each time, you can keep it fresh with format-based prompts:

"Suggest an episode of a horror anthology told entirely from the point of view of a house."

"Give me a sci-fi story idea that takes place in real time, over the course of 30 minutes."

"What's a romantic tragedy episode that plays out in reverse chronological order?"

For a comedy series, you can generate plots that balance humor with chaos:

"Give me a sitcom episode idea where a small lie spirals into a town-wide misunderstanding."

"Suggest a comedic plot where a character takes a new job for the wrong reason."

"What's a bottle episode idea that creates conflict among roommates during a blackout?"

Want to experiment with style or structure? You can go meta:

"Suggest an episode where the characters realize they're in a TV show."

"Give me a story idea that breaks the fourth wall and challenges the audience's expectations."

"What's a nonlinear episode structure that could reveal hidden character motivations?"

If you have an existing pilot and want to brainstorm the next few episodes, you can say:

"Based on this pilot summary, suggest three episode ideas that continue the story and deepen the conflict."

"How can I escalate the stakes in episode two of a detective series where the protagonist is hiding something from their partner?"

You can also challenge ChatGPT to surprise you:

"Give me a totally unexpected twist for episode four of a survival drama."

"What's a story that flips the genre expectations halfway through the episode?"

"Write an episode idea where the villain turns out to be the victim."

When you land on an episode idea you like, you can ask for more detail:

"Expand this idea into a three-act outline."

"What are the emotional turning points in this story?"

"Write a scene-by-scene breakdown of this episode with character arcs included."

In the world of television writing, ideas are your currency—and with the right ChatGPT prompts, you've got a printing press. Whether you're crafting full seasons or just trying to get to the next beat, prompting gives you endless momentum, unexpected twists, and layered stories that feel alive and binge-able.

Every episode starts with a question. The right prompt makes sure the answer is something worth watching.

Examples of ChatGPT Prompts for Character Ideas

Strong characters are the heart of every unforgettable series. They drive the story forward, embody its themes, and give the audience someone to root for, love, hate, or obsess over. But coming up with fresh, layered, and dynamic characters—especially across an ensemble cast—can be tricky. Sometimes you've got a vibe in mind but no name. Sometimes you've got a function in the plot, but no personality. That's where ChatGPT becomes an insanely useful tool. With the right prompts, you can build compelling protagonists, antagonists, love interests, sidekicks, mentors, rivals, and more. All with specific motivations, flaws, contradictions, and arcs that feel alive from the start.

Let's begin with some open-ended character creation prompts:

"Create a unique protagonist for a sci-fi drama series about memory manipulation."

"Give me five character ideas for a small-town crime thriller ensemble."

"Invent a complex antagonist for a legal drama who believes they're the hero."

"Suggest a love interest who challenges the main character's worldview in a coming-of-age series."

These work great when you're looking for fresh inspiration. You can narrow things down by adding tone, age, identity, or archetype:

"Give me a morally gray female lead in her 40s for a psychological mystery."

"Create a comic relief character for a workplace comedy, but make them emotionally deep."

"Invent a teenage sidekick who's wise beyond their years but emotionally guarded."

"Suggest a mentor character for a fantasy series who hides a dark secret."

If you already have a show concept, you can generate a character to *fit* into your world:

"I'm writing a dystopian thriller about rebels in a flooded city—give me a main character who's trying to keep their family safe."

"My show is about a group of roommates who start a cult by accident—who is the least likely cult leader?"

"Suggest a mysterious character who appears in episode three of a survival drama and shifts the group dynamic."

You can also prompt for specific **traits and dynamics**:

"Create a character who is incredibly charismatic but afraid of being alone."

"Give me a character who always tells the truth, even when it hurts others."

"Invent two characters who are complete opposites but forced to work together."

"Describe a character who thinks they're the smartest person in the room—but isn't."

Want to explore **flaws and contradictions**? Try:

"Give me a protagonist whose greatest strength is also their biggest flaw."

"Create a character who is deeply kind but terrible at confrontation."

"Invent a villain who is driven by love, not hate."

"Describe a hero who's terrified of success."

If you have a character idea already, you can expand on it:

"I have a character who's a reclusive hacker—what's their backstory, personality, and arc?"

"My protagonist is a former child star trying to go straight. What internal conflicts might they face?"

"What does my antagonist secretly want but can't admit to anyone—not even themselves?"

You can also build **relationships** using prompts:

"Describe a complex sibling relationship where one is successful and the other lives in their shadow."

"What kind of love interest would challenge my main character's fear of vulnerability?"

"Give me a foil character who reveals the flaws in my protagonist's approach to life."

"Create a best friend character who's loyal, but starting to grow apart from the lead."

For ensembles, try this:

"I need five distinct characters for a heist crew. Make each one unique in personality, skill, and motivation."

"Give me six main characters for a dramedy about a dysfunctional family who run a bed and breakfast."

"Create an ensemble cast for a political thriller, with a balance of heroes, antiheroes, and wildcards."

When you're worldbuilding or working in genre, characters should reflect the environment. Try:

"Invent a character for a post-apocalyptic series who refuses to let go of the old world."

"Give me a character for a space opera who's allergic to authority but brilliant at strategy."

"Create a witch character for a magical realism series who denies her own power."

Want deeper **psychological detail**? Ask:

"Describe a character's core fear and how it shapes every decision they make."

"Give me a protagonist who's haunted by something they did five years ago."

"What secret does this character keep from everyone, and why?"

"How does this character's upbringing affect their ability to trust people?"

You can also roleplay with ChatGPT to *get to know* your character:

"Let's do a character interview. I'll ask questions, and you answer as this character."

"You're my protagonist. What do you want most in the world—and what's stopping you?"

"What does your character regret the most, and how do they hide it?"

And when you're done building your characters, you can say:

"Write a short character breakdown for a pitch deck."

"Summarize this character's arc over the course of the first season."

"Describe this character's visual style and how they'd appear on screen."

Every show needs unforgettable characters—people we can love, fight with, laugh at, cry for, and grow alongside. The right ChatGPT prompt can take a half-baked idea and turn it into someone who feels *real*. Someone who doesn't just move through the story, but *drives* it. Someone you can't wait to write for.

Because stories are built on characters—and characters are built one great prompt at a time.

I hope you found inspiration within these pages. If you liked this book, please leave a review where you bought it. Thank you from the author.

www.ingramcontent.com/pod-product-compliance
Lightning Source LLC
LaVergne TN
LVHW082349200926
848481LV00012B/3509